Men with Adult ADHD 5-in-1

Master Focus, Productivity, and Your Emotions with CBT Tools to Improve Executive Function, Organization, Time Management and Relationships

JAREN KNOX

© Copyright 2025 - All rights reserved.

The content contained within this book may not be reproduced, duplicated, or transmitted without direct written permission from the author or the publisher.

Under no circumstances will any blame or legal responsibility be held against the publisher or author for any damages, reparation, or monetary loss due to the information contained within this book, either directly or indirectly.

Legal Notice: This book is copyright protected. It is only for personal use. You cannot amend, distribute, sell, use, quote, or paraphrase any part, or the content within this book, without the consent of the author or publisher.

Disclaimer Notice: Please note the information contained within this document is for educational and entertainment purposes only. All effort has been executed to present accurate, up-to-date, reliable, complete information. No warranties of any kind are declared or implied. Readers acknowledge that the author is not engaged in the rendering of legal, financial, medical, or professional advice. The content within this book has been derived from various sources. Please consult a licensed professional before attempting any techniques outlined in this book.

By reading this document, the reader agrees that under no circumstances is the author responsible for any losses, direct or indirect, that are incurred as a result of the use of the information contained within this document, including, but not limited to, errors, omissions, or inaccuracies.

DEDICATION

To every man facing the daily challenges of Adult ADHD. May this book be a guide, a toolkit, and a testament to your inherent strength and limitless potential. Your journey matters.

FOREWORD BY CAROLINA ESTEVEZ, PSY.D.

Men with Adult ADHD 5-in-1: Master Focus, Productivity, and Your Emotions with CBT Tools to Improve Executive Function, Organization, Time Management and Relationships by Jaren Knox is an exceptional and empowering handbook for men facing the challenges of ADHD. This book addresses the unique challenges that men with attention, concentration, and memory concerns face every day—such as managing impulsivity, disorganization, emotional reactivity, and inconsistent focus—through practical and evidence-based Cognitive Behavioral

Therapy (CBT) tools.

What sets this book apart is its clear, relatable tone and structured approach to helping readers build executive functioning skills. The strategies for improving focus, time management, and emotional regulation are not only rooted in research, but are also highly actionable and tailored to real-life situations that adult men often encounter, both professionally and personally.

As a psychologist, I appreciate how the book balances skill-building with emotional insight, acknowledging the frustration, shame, and self-doubt that frequently accompany undiagnosed or untreated ADHD. The guidance on improving relationships and self-awareness helps clients reframe their struggles and feel empowered rather than defeated. I would wholeheartedly recommend this book to clients because it offers a sense of clarity and direction, and it can complement therapy sessions by reinforcing skills that are learned and practiced in sessions. For men seeking to take control of their ADHD and create lasting change, this book provides a practical roadmap that is both motivating and accessible.

TABLE OF CONTENTS

INTRODUCTION 1

BOOK ONE: STRENGTHENING EXECUTIVE FUNCTION: THE BRAIN'S COMMAND CENTER 5

    CHAPTER 1: UNDERSTANDING EXECUTIVE BRAIN FUNCTION IN MEN WITH ADHD 7

    CHAPTER 2: ENHANCING WORKING MEMORY AND ATTENTION 14

    CHAPTER 3: MASTERING PLANNING AND PRIORITIZATION 25

    CHAPTER 4: CULTIVATING TASK INITIATION AND FOLLOW-THROUGH 34

    CHAPTER 5: DEVELOPING SELF-REGULATION AND IMPULSE CONTROL 44

    CONCLUSION: YOUR SHARPENED MIND 54

BOOK TWO: MASTERING FOCUS: SUSTAINED ATTENTION IN A DISTRACTING WORLD 57

    CHAPTER 1: UNDERSTANDING THE ADHD FOCUS CHALLENGE 59

    CHAPTER 2: ENVIRONMENTAL DESIGN FOR FOCUS 66

    CHAPTER 3: MINDFULNESS AND PRESENCE FOR ATTENTION 74

    CHAPTER 4: SINGLE-TASKING AND DEEP WORK STRATEGIES 81

    CHAPTER 5: SUSTAINING FOCUS AND PREVENTING BURNOUT 88

    CONCLUSION: YOUR FOCUSED EDGE 95

BOOK THREE: UNLEASHING PRODUCTIVITY: TURNING INTENTIONS INTO ACCOMPLISHMENTS 97

    CHAPTER 1: REDEFINING PRODUCTIVITY FOR ADHD MEN 99

    CHAPTER 2: TASK BREAKDOWN AND ACTIONABLE STEPS 104

    CHAPTER 3: OVERCOMING PROCRASTINATION AND RESISTANCE 111

    CHAPTER 4: WORKFLOW OPTIMIZATION AND SYSTEM BUILDING 119

    CHAPTER 5: REVIEW, ADAPT, AND ITERATE 127

    CONCLUSION: YOUR PRODUCTIVE POWER 135

BOOK FOUR: MASTERING YOUR EMOTIONS WITH CBT TOOLS: NAVIGATING THE INNER LANDSCAPE 137

- INTRODUCTION: THE EMOTIONAL ROLLERCOASTER AND YOUR GUIDING HAND 139
- CHAPTER 1: THE EMOTIONAL LANDSCAPE OF ADULT ADHD 142
- CHAPTER 2: IDENTIFYING AND CHALLENGING DISTORTED THOUGHTS (CBT) 148
- CHAPTER 3: BEHAVIORAL STRATEGIES FOR EMOTIONAL REGULATION (CBT) 156
- CHAPTER 4: BUILDING EMOTIONAL RESILIENCE AND DISTRESS TOLERANCE (CBT) 164
- CHAPTER 5: COMPASSIONATE SELF-TALK AND INNER DIALOGUE 169
- CONCLUSION: YOUR EMOTIONAL STRENGTH 174

BOOK FIVE: ORGANIZATION, TIME MANAGEMENT, AND RELATIONSHIPS: CRAFTING A BALANCED LIFE 177

- CHAPTER 1: ORGANIZING YOUR PHYSICAL AND DIGITAL WORLD 179
- CHAPTER 2: TIME MANAGEMENT STRATEGIES FOR THE ADHD BRAIN 184
- CHAPTER 3: NURTURING RELATIONSHIPS AND COMMUNICATION 189
- CHAPTER 4: SELF-CARE AND PREVENTING BURNOUT IN A DEMANDING WORLD 194
- CONCLUSION: YOUR BALANCED LIFE, REDEFINED 199

OVERALL CONCLUSION: THE EMPOWERED MAN WITH ADHD 201

INTRODUCTION

You've likely felt it: the relentless hum of a mind that won't quiet, the struggle to initiate tasks even when you know their importance, or the frustration of seeing your best intentions derailed by disorganization or a racing clock.

Perhaps you've been told to "just focus harder," "try to be more organized," or "get it together," all while feeling an unseen battle raging within. This internal landscape, often misunderstood and mislabeled, is the unique experience of Adult ADHD in men, and it can feel like trying to navigate a dense fog with a compass that spins wildly.

Building on that, this internal struggle is not just a personal feeling but a scientifically recognized condition with measurable impacts. For instance, studies show that men are more frequently diagnosed with ADHD than women, with one study finding the prevalence to be 5.4% in men versus 3.2% in women, although the gender gap narrows in adulthood (Montare Behavioral Health). This is often because men are more likely to exhibit the hyperactive and impulsive symptoms that lead to an earlier diagnosis.

The consequences of undiagnosed or unmanaged ADHD extend beyond daily frustrations and can significantly affect a man's quality of life and occupational and social functioning. Men with ADHD, for example, are at a higher risk for adverse outcomes in their daily lives. Research indicates that drivers with ADHD are more likely to have a license revoked, receive multiple traffic citations, and be involved in serious car crashes. One study from Sweden's Karolinska Institute found that men with ADHD who are not receiving treatment are up to 47% more likely to be involved in a car accident (Mark Salomone). Furthermore, the link between ADHD and the criminal justice system is striking. As many as 1 in 4 people in prison have been diagnosed with ADHD, which is more than eight times the rate in the general population (WebMD). This underscores the critical need to understand and manage this condition.

For too long, the narrative around ADHD has focused on childhood hyperactivity or the simplistic notion of "lacking attention." But for adult men, the manifestation is often far more nuanced: a complex interplay of executive function challenges, emotional dysregulation, and a pervasive sense of overwhelm that impacts careers, relationships, and self-esteem. You might excel in bursts of hyperfocus, only to crash into walls of procrastination. You may possess brilliant ideas, yet struggle to translate them into consistent action. And the emotional swings can feel isolating, leaving you feeling frustrated and alone.

A paradox lives in this struggle: the very strategies you've employed to control, fix, or suppress your ADHD symptoms may have inadvertently intensified them. The harder you've pushed for perfection, the more anxiety may have swelled. The more you've tried to force focus, the more your mind may have resisted. True mastery doesn't come from battling your brain, but from understanding it, honoring its unique wiring, and equipping it with the right tools.

This book is your comprehensive toolkit, a 5-in-1 guide meticulously crafted to address the core areas where men with Adult ADHD often seek greater mastery. Drawing on effective Cognitive Behavioral Therapy (CBT) principles, alongside practical, actionable strategies, we will navigate:

- **Executive Function:** Sharpening your planning, prioritization, and decision-making skills.
- **Focus:** Cultivating sustained attention and minimizing everyday distractions.
- **Productivity:** Transforming intentions into consistent output and achieving meaningful goals.
- **Emotional Regulation:** Understanding and managing intense emotions, irritability, and rejection sensitivity.
- **Organization, Time Management & Relationships:** Building practical systems for order, optimizing your schedule, and fostering stronger, more fulfilling connections.

Your journey towards a more focused, productive, emotionally balanced, and connected life begins now. You possess an incredible capacity for growth and adaptation. All you need is the right map and the right tools.

BOOK ONE:
STRENGTHENING EXECUTIVE FUNCTION:
THE BRAIN'S COMMAND CENTER

CHAPTER 1:

UNDERSTANDING EXECUTIVE BRAIN FUNCTION IN MEN WITH ADHD

Imagine your brain as a highly sophisticated command center, constantly processing information, making decisions, and directing your actions. At the heart of this command center lies what scientists call executive function. Think of it as the air traffic controller of your mind, responsible for managing your thoughts, emotions, and behaviors to achieve your goals. It's what helps you plan your day, stay focused on a task, remember important details, and resist distractions. More formally, executive functions are a set of cognitive skills that include:

Working Memory: The ability to hold information in your mind and use it to complete a task. It's like your mental scratchpad. For men with ADHD, working memory can sometimes feel like a sieve, allowing crucial details to slip away. This isn't a deficit in intelligence but a difference in how the brain retains and manipulates information short-term. Challenges might manifest as forgetting what you were about to say mid-sentence, misplacing items immediately after using them, or struggling to follow multi-step instructions without constant reminders.

Enhancing working memory isn't about brute force memorization but developing strategies to offload cognitive burden, such as note-taking, using visual aids, or breaking down complex tasks into smaller, more manageable parts that require less simultaneous mental juggling. We'll delve into specific techniques, from active recall exercises to utilizing external memory aids, designed to solidify your mental "scratchpad" and make information more readily accessible when you need it most. These foundational working memory skills impact nearly every other executive function. Strengthening your working memory is a cornerstone of improved daily performance.

Flexible Thinking: The capacity to shift gears, adapt to new situations, and consider different perspectives. For many men with ADHD, a rigid thought pattern or a tendency to get "stuck" on a particular idea or approach can be a significant hurdle. This might mean difficulty transitioning between tasks, struggling to adjust plans when unexpected obstacles arise, or finding it hard to see a situation from someone else's point of view, particularly in social interactions. This inflexibility can lead to frustration when routines are disrupted or when a planned outcome doesn't materialize. Developing flexible thinking involves consciously challenging your initial assumptions, practicing problem-solving from multiple angles, and cultivating an openness to change.

It's about building mental agility, allowing you to pivot gracefully in response to life's inevitable twists and turns, whether it's a sudden change in work priorities or an unforeseen social engagement. We'll explore methods to deliberately practice cognitive flexibility, encouraging you to embrace novelty and reframe setbacks as opportunities for creative solutions.

Self-Control/Inhibition: The power to resist impulses, override automatic responses, and pause before acting. This executive function is often profoundly impacted in men with ADHD, leading to impulsive decisions, interruptions in conversation, or difficulty delaying gratification. Whether it's blurting out thoughts without considering the consequences, overspending on a whim, or getting drawn into immediate distractions instead of focusing on long-term goals, challenges in self-control can have wide-ranging implications. This isn't a moral or self-control related failure, but a neurobiological deficit in the brain's "stop" signals.

Learning to strengthen inhibitory control involves recognizing triggers for impulsive behavior, developing a pause-and-plan mechanism, and practicing mindful responses. We will cover strategies like the "STOP" technique (Stop, Think, Observe, Proceed) and cultivating a greater awareness of your internal states to allow for more deliberate, rather than reactive, choices. This enhanced ability to inhibit unwanted behaviors is critical for fostering healthier relationships, making sound financial decisions, and maintaining focus on important tasks.

Planning and Prioritization: The skill of organizing tasks, setting goals, and determining the most important steps. For men with ADHD, the process of breaking down large projects into manageable steps, estimating time accurately, and ranking tasks by urgency and importance can be overwhelming. This often results in a sense of paralysis, an inability to start, or a tendency to focus on less important, more engaging tasks while critical deadlines loom. The challenge isn't a lack of desire to plan but a difficulty in the sequential and hierarchical thinking required.

Effective planning involves understanding your energy cycles, creating realistic timelines, and utilizing visual tools to map out your objectives. We will introduce frameworks for robust planning, such as backward planning from a deadline, and various prioritization matrices (e.g., Eisenhower Matrix) that help cut through the noise and identify truly high-leverage activities. This mastery of planning transforms vague intentions into concrete action steps, providing a clear roadmap for achieving your ambitions.

Task Initiation: The ability to start tasks without excessive procrastination. This is a common and often agonizing hurdle for men with ADHD. Despite knowing what needs to be done, the gap between intention and action can feel immense, leading to significant delays and missed opportunities. This isn't laziness but often a struggle with perceived effort, fear of failure, or a lack of immediate reward. The "just start" advice often falls flat because the neurological mechanism for initiating action is affected.

We'll explore techniques to reduce the friction of starting, such as the "five-minute rule," body doubling, breaking tasks into minuscule "micro-steps," and building motivational cues. Understanding the specific barriers to initiation, be it overwhelm, perfectionism, or distraction, allows for targeted interventions that make starting feel less like climbing a mountain and more like stepping onto a gentle slope. Cultivating strong task initiation habits unlocks productivity and reduces the mental burden of uninitiated work or tasks awaiting action.

Organization: The systematic arrangement of information, thoughts, and physical items. A common challenge for men with ADHD is maintaining order in both their physical environment and their mental landscape. This can manifest as cluttered workspaces, disorganized digital files, chaotic schedules, or difficulty categorizing thoughts during problem-solving. Disorganization isn't merely untidiness; it's a significant drain on executive function, as constant searching for items or information consumes valuable mental energy and time.

We will explore practical strategies for creating intuitive organizational systems, from "a place for everything and everything in its place" for physical items to digital file management and effective note-taking methods for thoughts and information. The goal is to create external structures that support your internal executive functions, reducing cognitive load and freeing up mental resources for higher-level tasks. An organized system creates predictable pathways, minimizing distractions and maximizing efficiency.

Monitoring: The capacity to check your work, track your progress, and adjust as needed. This executive function involves self-awareness and continuous self-assessment. For men with ADHD, challenges in monitoring can lead to overlooking errors, misjudging the impact of their actions, or struggling to adapt strategies that aren't working. It's the "feedback loop" of the brain that helps you learn from experience and refine your approach. This might mean difficulty staying on track during a task, failing to notice when your attention drifts, or not recognizing when a conversation is going awry. Improving monitoring involves cultivating metacognition (thinking about your thinking) and implementing checkpoints throughout your tasks and day.

We will discuss methods for self-correction, reviewing progress against goals, and developing a heightened awareness of your own cognitive and emotional states. Effective monitoring transforms your experiences into valuable learning opportunities, enabling you to continuously refine your strategies and achieve consistent improvement.

For men with ADHD, the ability to self-monitor operates a bit differently. While the core machinery is all there, signals might sometimes get crossed, priorities might shift unexpectedly, or impulse control might take an unscheduled coffee break. Perhaps you've experienced the frustration of knowing exactly what you need to do but you struggle to start it or you've found yourself constantly side-tracked by incoming emails, notifications, or a sudden, compelling idea. Maybe keeping track of appointments feels like a constant battle, or organizing your workspace (physical or digital) seems insurmountable. These experiences are not uncommon and are deeply rooted in the neurobiology of ADHD, leading to a pervasive sense of being overwhelmed, constantly playing catch-up, and feeling as though your potential is hindered by internal resistance. The mental fatigue that accompanies these struggles is substantial, often leading to burnout and a cycle of self-criticism.

This isn't a sign of weakness or a lack of intelligence; it's simply how your brain is wired. Research shows that ADHD involves differences in brain structure and neurotransmitter activity, particularly in areas of the prefrontal cortex: the very region responsible for executive functions. Specifically, there are often variations in the density and function of dopamine and norepinephrine pathways, which are critical for regulating attention, motivation, reward, and impulse control.

These neurochemical differences can explain why tasks that require sustained effort, planning, or inhibition feel disproportionately challenging. You're not alone in this experience, and understanding why these challenges arise is the first crucial step toward addressing them. Recognizing ADHD as a neurodevelopmental difference, rather than a character flaw, is profoundly liberating. It shifts the narrative from "I'm not trying hard enough" to "My brain works differently, and I need specific tools to help it operate optimally." This understanding paves the way for self-compassion and effective strategy development.

We're going to dive into the intricate workings of the executive brain, specifically through the lens of adult ADHD in men. We'll explore how challenges in areas like working memory, attention, planning, task initiation, and self-regulation can impact daily life, from professional endeavors to personal relationships. From missed deadlines and forgotten errands to difficulty managing anger or sticking to a budget, the ripple effects of executive function differences can be profound and often lead to feelings of overwhelm, frustration, or even shame. Consider the professional sphere: a brilliant idea stalled by procrastination, a promotion missed due to disorganization, or strained collegial relationships from impulsive remarks.

In personal life, it could be the frustration of a partner over forgotten promises, the chaos of a perpetually messy home, or the guilt associated with unfulfilled intentions. This book aims to dismantle those feelings by providing clarity and actionable solutions, not by masking symptoms, but by building robust internal and external systems that support your unique brain wiring. We will move beyond merely identifying problems to proactively constructing a life that leverages your strengths and mitigates your challenges.

More importantly, we'll begin to lay the groundwork for a new understanding of your own brain, recognizing its unique strengths while identifying areas where targeted strategies can make a profound difference.

This isn't about "fixing" ADHD. It's a neurodevelopmental difference rooted in the brain's unique wiring and chemistry. While ADHD impacts everyone differently, its core lies in variations in how certain brain regions, particularly those in the prefrontal cortex (the brain's executive control center), communicate and how neurotransmitters like dopamine and norepinephrine are regulated. These neurotransmitters are crucial for attention, motivation, reward, and impulse control.

For individuals with ADHD, these systems may not function optimally, leading to the well-known challenges of the condition. Understanding this underlying neurobiology is crucial because it shifts the perspective from a moral failing to a recognition of a genuine neurological difference. This perspective empowers you to approach your challenges with curiosity and strategic thinking, rather than self-blame. It enables you to see your brain not as broken, but as a uniquely wired instrument that requires a specific instruction manual and maintenance schedule to perform at its best.

In the chapters to come, we'll break down each of these executive functions, offering practical, evidence-based strategies tailored specifically for the ADHD brain. You'll learn how to bolster your working memory, sharpen your attention, master the art of planning, overcome procrastination, and cultivate greater self-control. We will equip you with a comprehensive toolkit that includes Cognitive Behavioral Therapy (CBT) informed techniques, practical organizational hacks, and mindfulness practices, all designed to create sustainable change. Each strategy will be presented with clear explanations, relatable examples, and actionable steps you can implement immediately.

Get ready to embark on a journey that will empower you to become the architect of your own mind, transforming challenges into opportunities for growth and success. This journey is not about eradicating ADHD, but about building a life where your neurodiversity becomes a source of unique strengths and adaptive capabilities. The command center of your mind and behaviors is yours to master and lead, and with the right tools, you will navigate it with unprecedented clarity and control.

CHAPTER 2:

ENHANCING WORKING MEMORY AND ATTENTION

In the grand scheme of your brain's command center, working memory and attention are two of the most critical operators. They work in tandem, constantly interacting to help you process information, stay on task, and make sense of the world around you. For men with ADHD, these two functions often present unique challenges, and developing specific strategies to enhance them can dramatically improve daily functioning and reduce frustration.

This chapter will illuminate the intricate interplay between working memory and attention, offering actionable, evidence-based techniques to sharpen these vital cognitive skills. Understanding their individual mechanisms and how they are impacted by ADHD is the first step toward reclaiming control over your mental focus and capacity. We will delve into the latest research insights, translating complex neuroscience into practical, everyday applications that resonate with the experiences of adult men navigating ADHD. The goal is not just to manage symptoms but to cultivate robust cognitive habits that foster greater efficiency, clarity, and confidence in all aspects of your life.

The Power of Working Memory: Your Brain's Mental Scratchpad

Think of working memory as your brain's temporary holding area: a mental scratchpad where you actively hold and manipulate information for a short period. It's what you use when someone gives you a phone number and you hold it in your mind just long enough to dial it, or when you're following a recipe and remembering the ingredients you've already added. It's crucial for understanding complex instructions, solving problems, and even following conversations. Without a robust working memory, even simple daily tasks can become arduous, leading to errors, forgotten details, and a pervasive sense of being overwhelmed. Consider the cumulative effect of constantly having to re-read instructions, re-ask questions, or retrace your steps; this cognitive friction drains energy and erodes confidence.

For men with ADHD, this "mental scratchpad" is often prone to glitches. It's not that the capacity isn't there, but rather that the information might not "stick" long enough or might be easily overwritten by new stimuli. This isn't a deficit in intelligence or effort, but a characteristic of how the ADHD brain processes and retains transient information, often due to differences in neural pathways involving neurotransmitters like dopamine and norepinephrine that are vital for information processing and retention.

For men with ADHD, a common experience is that this mental scratchpad can feel more like a sieve. Information goes in, but it often slips out before it can be fully processed or stored. This can manifest as:

- **Difficulty remembering instructions**: You hear them, but they vanish moments later. You might nod along, fully intending to comply, only to find the specific details have evaporated when you go to execute the task. This can lead to frustration from supervisors, colleagues, or partners who may misinterpret this as disinterest or incompetence. The internal experience, however, is one of acute blankness, a "tip-of-the-tongue" sensation for information that was just presented.
- **Struggling to follow multi-step tasks**: You get lost halfway through. Imagine trying to assemble furniture from a detailed diagram or cook a complex meal; each step seems to overwrite the previous one, forcing you to constantly refer back to the instructions, which itself becomes a taxing act on working memory. This often leads to incomplete projects, errors, and significant time overruns.
- **Losing your train of thought in conversations**: You forget what you were going to say or what the other person just said. This can make reciprocal conversations feel like a high-wire act, leading to awkward pauses, accidental interruptions, or the inability to contribute meaningfully to a discussion. It impacts social connections and professional interactions, as others may perceive you as inattentive or disengaged.
- **Challenges with mental math or complex reasoning**: Holding numbers or ideas in mind feels overwhelming. Simple calculations, comparing options, or synthesizing information from multiple sources can become a Herculean effort if you cannot reliably hold the necessary data in your short-term mental buffer. This impacts decision-making, problem-solving, and your ability to engage in strategic thinking.

These manifestations are not indicators of your overall intellectual capacity but rather signal specific points of friction within your working memory system. The good news is that just as you can train a muscle, you can implement strategies to bolster your working memory, compensating for inherent differences and building more robust systems for information retention and retrieval.

Strategies to Bolster Your Working Memory

Externalize Everything: Your brain isn't the best place for storage. Get the information out! Use notebooks, sticky notes, whiteboards, or digital tools (apps like Evernote, Google Keep, or Trello) to capture ideas, to-do lists, and crucial information immediately. The act of writing or typing helps solidify the information, and having it externalized frees up your working memory for active processing.

This is perhaps the single most impactful strategy for working memory challenges. Instead of relying on your internal "scratchpad," which is prone to erasure, create an external, durable one. This means immediately jotting down ideas that pop into your head, capturing instructions verbatim, documenting decisions, and maintaining comprehensive to-do lists. The specific tool doesn't matter as much as the habit of consistent, immediate externalization. For physical items, consider a dedicated inbox for documents, a hook for keys, or a consistent spot for your wallet. The less your working memory has to hold onto, the more capacity it has for the active processing required for problem-solving and immediate tasks. This also reduces anxiety, as you no longer have to fear forgetting something important.

Break It Down: Complex tasks overwhelm working memory. Deconstruct large projects into smaller, manageable steps. If you have to remember five things, break them into five separate, smaller "chunks" that are easier to hold. This strategy is critical for avoiding cognitive overload. When faced with a large project like "organize the garage" or "prepare for the annual review," the sheer scope can paralyze working memory, making it impossible to even begin. Instead, break it down: "clear a 2x2 foot section of the garage," "gather last year's performance review," or "outline the main points of my contribution."

Each smaller step requires less simultaneous mental effort and feels more approachable. For instructions, ask for them to be given one or two steps at a time, or immediately write down each step as it's provided. This reduces the burden on your mental scratchpad, allowing you to focus on executing one "chunk" before moving to the next.

Visualize It: If you're trying to remember a sequence or a list, try to create a mental image or a story connecting the items. For example, if you need to buy milk, bread, and eggs, picture a cow drinking milk, eating bread, and laying eggs. The more vivid and unusual, the better. Our brains are incredibly adept at remembering images and stories. By transforming abstract information (like a list of items or a sequence of instructions) into a concrete, often absurd, mental picture, you're tapping into a more primal and resilient memory system. This is why memory champions use elaborate "memory palaces."

While you don't need to build a palace for your grocery list, a simple, vivid visualization can significantly improve recall. If you have to remember a series of steps for a procedure, imagine yourself performing them, perhaps with exaggerated or humorous movements. This active mental engagement encodes the information more deeply than passive listening.

Use Repetition and Elaboration: When you receive new information, repeat it aloud or to yourself. Then, try to elaborate on it or connect it to something you already know. For instance, if you're introduced to "John Smith," you might think, "John Smith, like the explorer." This active processing helps solidify the memory. This technique leverages the principle that active engagement with information strengthens its neural pathways. Simply hearing something isn't enough; you need to process it. Repeating it aloud (or sub-vocally) forces your brain to re-encode the information. Elaboration takes it a step further: by linking new information to existing knowledge, you're creating a richer, more interconnected neural network, making the new information easier to retrieve. For example, if learning a new concept at work, try to explain it in your own words or think about how it applies to a past project. This deep processing transforms shallow, transient memories into more robust, accessible ones.

Minimize Cognitive Load: Reduce the number of things your working memory has to manage simultaneously. Close unnecessary tabs on your computer, put your phone away, and dedicate yourself to one task at a time when possible. Fewer inputs mean more capacity for the task at hand. In our hyper-connected world, we are constantly bombarded with stimuli. Each open tab, each notification, each background conversation is vying for a slice of your limited working memory.

For the ADHD brain, which already struggles with filtering, this constant barrage creates significant cognitive noise. By proactively reducing inputs, you create a clearer mental workspace. This might involve closing all but essential applications when working, designating specific "no-interruption" times, or even physically turning away from distracting environments. The goal is to funnel your mental resources into a single stream, allowing your working memory to operate at its full, albeit unique, capacity without being fragmented by competing demands.

"Chunking" Information: Group related pieces of information together. Phone numbers (e.g., 555-123-4567) are a classic example of chunking. Apply this principle to lists, concepts, or instructions. Instead of remembering seven individual digits for a phone number, we remember two chunks (a three-digit and a four-digit sequence, or three sets of three or four digits). This dramatically reduces the burden on working memory.

Apply this to other areas: if you have a list of errands, group them by location (e.g., "bank, post office, grocery store" as one "chunk" for the main street). If you're studying a topic, group related sub-topics together. This strategy makes large amounts of information more digestible and manageable for your working memory, transforming what feels like an endless stream of data into discrete, memorable units.

The effectiveness of this technique, known as "chunking," is a cornerstone of cognitive psychology, first popularized by George A. Miller in his 1956 paper, "The Magical Number Seven, Plus or Minus Two." Subsequent research has confirmed that chunking helps bypass the limited capacity of working memory by organizing information into meaningful groups. For example, a 2021 study on high school students found that those who used chunking to divide information into two or three groups were able to memorize and recall information significantly more effectively than those who were given the same information all at once (ResearchGate).

This ability to recode smaller units into a single, familiar chunk reduces cognitive load and frees up capacity for other information, leading to better overall retention and recall.

Sharpening Attention: Focusing Your Mental Spotlight

Attention is your mental spotlight, determining where your brain's resources are directed. It allows you to select relevant information and filter out distractions. For men with ADHD, this spotlight often behaves more like a disco ball, flitting rapidly from one stimulus to another, making it difficult to sustain focus on a single task, even one you find interesting. This isn't a lack of desire to focus, but a challenge in regulating the intensity and duration of the mental spotlight. The brain's filtering mechanisms, particularly in the prefrontal cortex, may struggle to prioritize relevant stimuli over irrelevant ones, leading to an almost equal weighting of all incoming information. This can be exhausting and lead to fragmented experiences, as your mind constantly pulls you in different directions. The insidious part of attention difficulties is that they often go unnoticed until a significant consequence (a missed deadline, a misunderstood instruction, an incomplete task) brings them to light.

This can lead to:

- **Difficulty initiating tasks**: The sheer volume of potential distractions makes starting hard. The very act of beginning a task requires a commitment of attention, but if your spotlight is constantly scanning for the next shiny object, it's hard to settle it on the task at hand. The decision paralysis stemming from a myriad of competing stimuli can be debilitating.
- **Frequent mind-wandering**: Your thoughts drift away from the task at hand. Even when you do manage to start, your internal landscape can be just as distracting as the external one. One thought leads to another, pulling your attention away from your intended focus, often without you even realizing it until minutes later.
- **Easily distracted by external stimuli**: A sound, a notification, or something visual pulls your attention away. The ADHD brain can be exquisitely sensitive to novel stimuli. A siren outside, a

phone vibrating, a person walking by; any of these can hijack your attention, pulling you away from what you're doing, sometimes for extended periods as you re-engage with the new stimulus.

- **Hyperfocus on less important tasks**: You might get intensely absorbed in something tangential while ignoring critical priorities. Paradoxically, the ADHD brain can also exhibit "hyperfocus," an intense absorption in a task that is often intrinsically interesting. While this sounds like a superpower, it becomes problematic when directed at non-priority tasks (e.g., meticulously organizing your sock drawer when a major work report is due). This is a form of attention dysregulation, not controlled focus.

Cultivating sustained attention requires intentional effort and the creation of an environment, both physical and mental, that supports focus. It's about training your mental spotlight to stay aimed, even when faced with compelling diversions.

Strategies to Cultivate Sustained Attention:

Create an "Attention Zone": Designate a specific physical space (even if it's just a corner of a room) that you associate only with focused work. Keep it tidy, free from distractions, and minimize visual clutter. This primes your brain to enter a state of focus when you're in that zone. The power of environmental cues cannot be overstated. By creating a dedicated "attention zone," you're building a psychological association between that space and focused activity.

This means no eating, no social media Browse, and ideally, no unrelated conversations in this specific area. The fewer competing associations that space has, the stronger its power to cue focus. Optimize lighting, minimize noise (noise-cancelling headphones can be a game-changer), and ensure comfortable ergonomics. This physical boundary helps create a mental one, signalling to your brain that "this is where deep work happens."

Time Blocking and the Pomodoro Technique: Allocate specific blocks of time for focused work (e.g., 25-minute intervals). During these blocks, commit to working on only one task, eliminating all distractions.

The Pomodoro Technique, developed by Francesco Cirillo in the late 1980s, involves 25 minutes of focused work followed by a 5-minute break. This structured approach trains your attention span. A study in *Time and Society* found that implementing the Pomodoro technique in a digital marketing company helped employees work more efficiently and improve their work-life balance (Pedersen et al., 2024). Time blocking means assigning specific tasks to specific time slots in your calendar. This prevents decision fatigue and provides a clear agenda.

The Pomodoro Technique breaks work into manageable sprints, leveraging the idea that sustained, intense focus is difficult beyond certain durations. The short breaks prevent burnout and allow for a mental reset. The structure provides external scaffolding for your attention, making the daunting prospect of "working all day" into a series of achievable, short focus bursts. During your focused "Pomodoros," put your phone on silent, close irrelevant tabs, and commit fully to the chosen task.

Single-Tasking: Resist the urge to multitask. While it might feel productive, switching between tasks rapidly depletes your attention and working memory. Focus on completing one thing before moving to the next. Multitasking is a myth for deep, meaningful work. What we perceive as multitasking is actually rapid task-switching, which incurs a "switching cost." Each time you jump from one task to another, your brain has to reorient itself, load relevant information into working memory, and discard the previous context. This process is inefficient and incredibly draining for the ADHD brain. Commit to true single-tasking: pick one item, and dedicate your full attention to it until it's complete or until your designated focus time ends. This practice dramatically improves the quality of your output and reduces the feeling of mental fragmentation.

Scheduled Distraction Breaks: Instead of fighting distractions, acknowledge them and schedule time for them. If a nagging thought or a desire to check social media arises, make a quick note of it and promise yourself you'll address it during your next scheduled break.

Trying to suppress every distracting thought or urge often backfires, increasing their intensity. Instead, use a "parking lot" approach: keep a notepad handy, and when a non-task-related thought pops up ("I need to call X," "Did I send that email?"), quickly jot it down and tell yourself you'll address it during your next scheduled break.

This validates the thought without letting it derail your current focus. Similarly, schedule specific times for checking email, social media, or news, rather than allowing them to constantly interrupt your flow. This creates boundaries for your attention, putting you in control rather than being at the mercy of external stimuli.

Active Listening and Engagement: In conversations, practice active listening by repeating or summarizing what the other person has said. This forces your attention to remain engaged and helps prevent mind-wandering.

For men with ADHD, conversations can be particularly challenging due to the interplay of working memory and attention. Active listening is a powerful antidote. When you actively summarize or reflect what the other person has said, you're not just proving you heard them; you're forcing your brain to process, encode, and momentarily hold their words in your working memory.

This acts as an "attention anchor," keeping your mental spotlight firmly on the conversation. It also ensures comprehension and builds stronger rapport. Practice asking clarifying questions, making eye contact, and resisting the urge to formulate your response while the other person is still speaking.

"Attention Anchors": Use subtle physical or sensory cues to bring your attention back. This could be a deep breath, focusing on your posture, or a specific object on your desk. When you notice your mind drifting, use your anchor to gently pull it back to the task. Attention anchors are mindful cues you can use to gently redirect your focus when you detect mind-wandering. A deep breath is a classic example: when your mind starts to drift, simply take a slow, deliberate inhale and exhale, bringing your awareness back to your body and then to the task.

You might choose a specific object on your desk, such as a pen, or a paperweight, to glance at and use as a visual cue to re-center. Alternatively, simply re-adjusting your posture can serve as a physical reminder to re-engage.

The key is to develop a consistent, simple anchor that you can deploy quickly and unobtrusively to bring your mental spotlight back to where you want it. This builds self-awareness and self-regulation.

Minimize Notifications: Turn off non-essential notifications on your phone and computer. Each chime or pop-up is a direct assault on your attention. Notifications are designed to hijack your attention.

For the ADHD brain, which is already prone to being externally distracted, they are particularly disruptive. Take ruthless control over your notifications. Turn off all non-essential alerts on your phone, tablet, and computer. For work-related apps, customize settings to only receive critical alerts.

Consider using "Do Not Disturb" modes during focused work periods. The fewer artificial "pings" your environment generates, the easier it will be for your brain to sustain its focus.

This simple act can dramatically reduce cognitive fragmentation and the constant urge to check your devices, freeing up significant mental bandwidth.

By understanding the distinct roles of working memory and attention, and by actively implementing these strategies, you can begin to strengthen these foundational executive functions.

It's a process of intentional training, much like building a muscle. The more you practice, the more resilient and effective your mental command center will become, setting the stage for greater control over your daily tasks and overall success. This journey requires patience and self-compassion.

There will be days when these strategies feel effortless, and days when they feel like an uphill battle. The key is consistent effort, acknowledging small victories, and adapting your approach as you learn what works best for your unique neurobiology.

The ultimate goal is to move from a reactive state, constantly battling distractions and forgetfulness, to a proactive one, where you are the conscious director of your attention and the master of your mental capacity.

You are equipping yourself not just to cope, but to thrive.

CHAPTER 3:

MASTERING PLANNING AND PRIORITIZATION

You have a destination in mind, but how do you get there efficiently, without getting lost or side tracked? This is where planning and prioritization come in. They are the GPS and the strategic map of your executive function command center. Planning is the ability to create a roadmap for achieving a goal, breaking it down into steps and anticipating potential obstacles. Prioritization is the skill of identifying which tasks are most important and urgent, ensuring your efforts are directed where they matter most.

These two skills, when harmonized, provide the crucial framework for converting intentions into tangible accomplishments. For men with ADHD, who often grapple with an internal landscape of competing thoughts and external environments rich with distractions, mastering planning and prioritization is not merely a convenience but a fundamental requirement for reducing overwhelm, enhancing productivity, and fostering a sense of control over one's life. The aim is to move beyond mere reactivity to a state of proactive purpose, where your actions are aligned with your deepest goals and values.

For men with ADHD, these skills can often feel like trying to navigate a dense fog with a faulty compass. The desire to achieve is strong, but the pathway to get there can be murky, leading to:

- **Difficulty initiating large projects**: The sheer scale of a task can be paralyzing without a clear plan. When a task appears as an undifferentiated monolith, the ADHD brain's executive functions, particularly task initiation, struggle to find an entry point. This leads to what's often called "analysis paralysis," where the magnitude of the work prevents any work from beginning at all. The internal dialogue can become a loop of "where do I even start?"
- **Underestimating time**: A tendency to believe tasks will take less time than they actually do, leading to last-minute rushes and missed deadlines. This optimistic bias, sometimes termed "time blindness," is a hallmark of ADHD. It's not intentional deception but a genuine difficulty in accurately perceiving and allocating time, leading to chronic lateness, hurried work, and the stress of always being behind schedule.
- **Getting side tracked by novelties**: The "shiny object" syndrome can derail a carefully laid plan in moments. The ADHD brain's heightened sensitivity to novelty means that new ideas, sudden inspirations, or unexpected stimuli can effortlessly pull attention away from current priorities, no matter how well-planned. This can result in a landscape of half-finished projects and forgotten intentions, as one fascinating tangent leads to another.
- **Struggling to differentiate between urgent and important**: Everything feels urgent, leading to a constant state of reactivity rather than proactive progress. When all incoming stimuli are perceived with similar weight, the capacity to discern true priorities is compromised. This results in a "fire-fighting" mentality, where immediate, often minor, demands consume all available energy, leaving critical long-term goals perpetually neglected.

- **Overwhelm and procrastination**: Without a clear path forward, it's easy to feel inundated and avoid starting altogether. The cumulative effect of these challenges is a deep sense of overwhelm. When the mental map is unclear, the compass is erratic, and every direction seems equally compelling yet daunting, the natural response for many is to simply avoid the journey, leading to significant procrastination and its accompanying guilt.

Mastering these functions isn't about rigid adherence to a perfect schedule, but about developing adaptable systems that work with your ADHD brain, not against it. It's about building external scaffolds that compensate for internal inconsistencies, creating a framework that supports your natural creativity and energy while providing the necessary structure to channel them effectively. These strategies are designed to provide clarity, reduce mental friction, and empower you to move forward with purpose, even when your internal wiring presents unique challenges.

Planning Your Route: Planning Your Route: Creating a Functional Roadmap

Effective planning for the ADHD brain needs to be visual, flexible, and broken down into digestible pieces. The linear, purely mental planning approach that works for some can be a significant barrier for others. By leveraging visual cues and externalizing cognitive load, you create a system that is more forgiving, adaptable, and intuitive for your brain's unique processing style. This approach acknowledges that the challenge isn't a lack of intelligence or capability, but a difference in how information is organized and accessed.

Strategies for Enhanced Planning:

The "Brain Dump" First: Before you can plan, you need to know everything that's occupying your mental space. Dedicate 10-15 minutes to write down everything you need to do, remember, or worry about. Don't filter, just get it all out. This clears your working memory and provides a raw inventory. This initial step is non-negotiable. Your working memory is a finite resource, and constantly juggling a mental list of tasks, worries, and ideas is incredibly draining. The brain dump provides immediate relief from this cognitive burden. Whether it's on a piece of paper, a digital document, or a whiteboard, the act of externalizing these thoughts allows your brain to release them temporarily, freeing up mental space for actual planning and problem-solving. This inventory also brings to light hidden tasks or anxieties that might unconsciously be contributing to your sense of overwhelm. Do this regularly, perhaps at the start or end of each day, or at the beginning of your weekly review.

Visual Planning Tools are Your Friends: Ditch purely mental plans. Utilize whiteboards, large paper calendars, digital mind-mapping tools (e.g., MindMeister, XMind), or project management apps (e.g., Trello, Asana). Seeing your tasks visually helps you connect the dots and anticipate steps.

For the ADHD brain, which often thinks in webs rather than linear lists, visual tools are invaluable. A large whiteboard where you can map out projects with sticky notes that can be moved around, a digital Kanban board in Trello showing tasks moving from "To Do" to "In Progress" to "Done," or a mind map illustrating the interconnectedness of ideas can make complex plans tangible and less intimidating. These tools leverage your brain's natural affinity for visual information, allowing you to see the entire scope of a project, identify dependencies, and track progress more intuitively. Experiment with different tools to find what resonates best with your personal style.

Reverse Engineering: For larger goals (e.g., "complete project X by end of month"), start at the deadline and work backward. What needs to be done the week before? The day before? This helps break down daunting tasks into smaller, actionable chunks. This strategy combats procrastination by changing your perspective. Instead of looking at a mountain of work, you're looking at the last small step needed to reach the summit, and then identifying the step just before that, and so on. This makes the initial steps less overwhelming and creates a clear sequence. For example, if you have a presentation due on Friday, what must be done by Thursday? What about Wednesday?

This helps identify critical milestones and prevents the last-minute panic that often accompanies time blindness. It also highlights potential bottlenecks early on, allowing you to adjust your plan before it's too late.

Estimate Realistically (and Add a Buffer): Acknowledge your tendency to underestimate time. For each task, estimate how long you think it will take, then add 25-50% more. This built-in buffer accounts for distractions, unexpected issues, or simply needing more time to get into "flow." This is a crucial self-awareness strategy. Time blindness is a real phenomenon in ADHD; you genuinely believe you can do something faster than you can. By consciously adding a buffer, you're building resilience into your schedule. This buffer isn't wasted time; it's an investment in your peace of mind and the quality of your work. It allows for interruptions, unexpected difficulties, and the natural fluctuations in your focus and energy. Over time, as you consistently add buffers and track your actual time, you'll develop a more accurate internal clock.

Identify the "Next Action": For every item on your list, ask yourself: "What's the very next physical action I need to take to move this forward?" Instead of "Plan vacation," the next action might be "Research flights to Bali" or "Ask a partner about preferred dates." This makes starting easier. This concept, popularized by David Allen in "Getting Things Done," is incredibly powerful for task initiation. "Plan vacation" is an overwhelming project, not an actionable step. By breaking it down to the smallest physical action (something you can *do*), you remove the mental barrier to starting. "Research flights to Bali" is a concrete action that can be performed. This micro-commitment lowers the activation energy required to begin, making procrastination less likely. Apply this relentlessly to every large, vague task on your list.

Schedule Transition Time: ADHD brains often struggle with transitions between tasks. Build in small breaks (5-10 minutes) between scheduled activities. This helps reset your focus and prevents the feeling of being constantly rushed. Transitions are points of friction for the ADHD brain.

Shifting from one task to a completely different one without a pause can be jarring and lead to mental "residue" from the previous activity, making it hard to engage with the next. Scheduling short breaks, even just to stand up, stretch, grab water, or look out a window, allows your brain to "reset." This isn't wasted time; it's an intentional re-calibration that primes you for the next period of focus. It reduces the feeling of being perpetually rushed and overwhelmed, which can trigger avoidance behaviors.

The "If-Then" Plan: Anticipate potential obstacles. For example: "IF I get distracted by emails while working on the report, THEN I will close my email client for the next 30 minutes." This pre-planned response reduces decision fatigue in the moment. The ADHD journey is filled with potential sidetracks and unexpected detours. "If-Then" planning (also known as implementation intentions) helps you preemptively navigate these. By deciding *in advance* how you will respond to common challenges, you eliminate the need for real-time decision-making when your executive functions might be compromised by distraction or emotional overwhelm.

This creates automatic, pre-programmed responses to triggers, making it easier to stay on track. Brainstorm your most common pitfalls (e.g., phone notifications, hunger, a sudden urge to clean) and create a corresponding "then" statement.

Prioritizing Your Efforts: Directing Your Focus

Not all tasks are created equal. Prioritization is about deciding what deserves your immediate attention versus what can wait or even be delegated. Without this skill, you risk spending all your energy on urgent but unimportant tasks, leaving the truly significant ones undone. For men with ADHD, the challenge often lies in the brain's tendency to give undue weight to novelty and immediate gratification, making it difficult to defer present desires for future rewards.

This means that an urgent email might feel more compelling than a long-term strategic project, even if the latter holds far greater importance. Developing robust prioritization skills shifts your focus from merely "doing things" to "doing the right things," aligning your efforts with your overarching goals and values. It moves you from a reactive state to one of deliberate, strategic action, significantly impacting your productivity and sense of accomplishment.

Strategies for Smarter Prioritization:

The Eisenhower Matrix: Categorize tasks into four quadrants:

- **Urgent & Important (Do First)**: Crises, deadlines, pressing problems. These tasks demand immediate attention and have significant consequences if neglected. For ADHD, these are often the tasks you feel compelled to address due to immediate pressure, but a healthy system minimizes the number of tasks in this quadrant through proactive planning.
- **Important, Not Urgent (Schedule)**: Planning, relationship building, prevention, long-term goals. This is where you want to spend most of your time. This quadrant is the powerhouse of strategic progress. These tasks are critical for your long-term success and well-being but often lack immediate external pressure, making them easy for the ADHD brain to defer. Deliberately scheduling time for these tasks is paramount.
- **Urgent, Not Important (Delegate/Minimize)**: Interruptions, some emails, minor requests. These tasks create a sense of urgency but contribute little to your core goals. For men with ADHD, these "urgent but unimportant" tasks can be particularly distracting due to their immediate demand for attention. Learn to identify them, delegate if possible, or address them quickly and efficiently without letting them derail your main focus.
- **Not Urgent, Not Important (Eliminate)**: Distractions, time-wasters. This framework provides a clear visual for decision-making. These are the activities that offer little to no value. For the ADHD brain, the allure of easy, low-effort activities in this quadrant can be a major time sink. Ruthlessly identify and eliminate them from your day. The Eisenhower Matrix is powerful because it forces you to think critically about the *value* of each task, not just its immediate pull.

Identify Your "Big Rocks": Before diving into your daily "pebbles" and "sand," identify the 1-3 most important tasks (your "big rocks") that must get done that day or week. Schedule these first. This ensures that even if other things go awry, your most critical priorities are addressed. This metaphor, often attributed to Stephen Covey, highlights the importance of proactive prioritization. If you fill your jar with sand (small, urgent tasks) and pebbles (medium-importance tasks) first, there will be no room for the big rocks (your most important goals). By scheduling and tackling your big rocks early in your most productive periods, you guarantee that what truly matters gets done, even if the rest of your day becomes chaotic. This creates a powerful sense of accomplishment and keeps you aligned with your long-term vision.

The "One Thing" Rule: Each day, pick one single task that, if completed, would make the biggest positive impact. Focus on that one thing, especially during your peak productive hours. This creates a sense of accomplishment and prevents overwhelm. This is a simplification of the "Big Rocks" concept, designed to be even more accessible for days when overwhelm feels imminent. By identifying just *one* crucial task, you reduce decision fatigue and concentrate your limited executive function on a single, high-leverage activity. Completing that one thing provides a significant psychological boost, reducing guilt and building momentum for future days. This is particularly effective for those days where getting started feels impossible; focusing on just one victory makes the day feel purposeful.

Consider Energy Levels: Don't just prioritize by importance; consider when you have the most energy and focus. Schedule your most demanding, "important-not-urgent" tasks during your peak productivity windows (e.g., mornings for many with ADHD), and save the less demanding tasks for times when your energy naturally dips. This is a critical adjustment for the ADHD brain. Your capacity for focused work fluctuates throughout the day. Trying to force intense concentration during a low-energy period is a recipe for frustration and procrastination. Learn to identify your personal "power hours": Times when you are naturally most alert and focused. Reserve these for your most challenging, high-impact tasks (Quadrant 2 of the Eisenhower Matrix). Use your lower-energy periods for administrative tasks, routine emails, or less cognitively demanding work. This leverages your natural rhythms rather than fighting against them.

Review and Adapt Daily/Weekly: Planning and prioritization aren't one-time events. At the end of each day or week, review what worked and what didn't. Did you underestimate time? Did you get side tracked? Adjust your approach for the next planning cycle. This iterative process is crucial for long-term improvement. Your brain is unique, and what works one week might need adjustment the next.

Regular review sessions (e.g., 15 minutes at the end of each day, an hour at the end of the week) allow you to objectively assess your strategies. Ask yourself: "What went well?" "What challenged me?" "What can I learn for tomorrow/next week?" This meta-cognition (in other words, thinking about your thinking) is essential for refining your planning and prioritization systems over time, making them increasingly tailored to your individual needs and patterns.

The 2-Minute Rule: If a task takes less than two minutes to complete, do it immediately. This prevents small, easy tasks from piling up and creating mental clutter that drains your executive function. This simple rule, also from "Getting Things Done," is a powerful antidote to procrastination of small tasks. Minor items such as replying to a quick email, filing a document, or putting away a dish can accumulate quickly, creating a background hum of unfinished business that saps mental energy.

By tackling them immediately, you prevent them from becoming "mental sticky notes" that constantly demand attention and drain your working memory. This frees up your cognitive resources for more significant tasks and provides small, consistent wins throughout your day.

By diligently applying these strategies, you'll transform planning from a source of anxiety into a powerful tool for clarity and direction.

You'll move beyond reacting to daily demands and start proactively shaping your days, ensuring your energy and attention are consistently directed towards what truly matters.

This mastery of planning and prioritization is a cornerstone of taking command of your executive brain, leading to increased productivity, reduced stress, and a greater sense of accomplishment in all areas of your life.

It is the framework upon which a more organized, purposeful, and fulfilling existence can be built, allowing your unique strengths to shine unhindered by the typical challenges of ADHD.

CHAPTER 4:

CULTIVATING TASK INITIATION AND FOLLOW-THROUGH

You've meticulously planned your day and prioritized your tasks, a truly commendable feat for any brain, let alone one with ADHD. But then comes the moment of truth: actually starting the thing, and then, perhaps even more challenging, sticking with it until it's done. This is where task initiation and follow-through step onto the stage as critical players in your executive function ensemble. These are the muscles of execution, translating your well-laid plans into tangible progress.

For many men with ADHD, the conceptualization of a task or goal is often effortless, even exciting. The initial burst of inspiration can be exhilarating. However, the chasm between having a brilliant idea or a clear to-do item and actually putting pen to paper (or fingers to keyboard, or body in motion) can feel impossibly wide. This is not a moral failing or a lack of will; it is a neurological hurdle, deeply intertwined with the brain's reward system and its ability to switch between modes of thinking and doing. Understanding this distinction is crucial to developing effective strategies that work *with* your brain's wiring, rather than constantly fighting against it.

Task initiation is the ability to begin a task without excessive delay, to bridge the gap between intention and action. It's the moment you overcome inertia and take that crucial first step. Follow-through, on the other hand, is the persistence to see a task through to completion, even when distractions arise or the initial novelty wears off. It's the sustained effort that transforms a good start into a finished product. For men with ADHD, these two areas are often significant stumbling blocks, manifesting as:

- **The "Just Can't Start" Syndrome**: You know exactly what you need to do, but an invisible wall seems to prevent you from taking that first step. The task feels overwhelming, uninteresting, or just… heavy. This is often described as "activation energy" deficiency. The brain struggles to generate the necessary internal "push" to shift from planning or contemplating to active engagement. The task may be perceived as too complex, too boring, or too effortful, leading to a state of mental paralysis despite a strong desire to begin.
- **Procrastination Spirals**: Delaying tasks until the last possible moment, often leading to rushed, lower-quality work and increased stress. Procrastination is a complex behavior, often serving as a coping mechanism for underlying challenges with task initiation, emotional regulation, or time perception. For men with ADHD, the looming pressure of an imminent deadline can sometimes provide the necessary dopamine rush to finally activate, but this "crisis management" approach is unsustainable, leading to chronic stress, missed opportunities, and a constant feeling of being behind.

- **The "Half-Finished" Project Pile**: A trail of abandoned tasks, half-read books, and partially completed hobbies, victims of dwindling interest or a new, more exciting idea. The initial novelty of a new project provides a dopamine hit, making initiation easier. However, as the task becomes routine or reaches a less stimulating phase, the inherent interest wanes, and the follow-through becomes incredibly challenging. The "shiny object" syndrome often pulls attention away to the next exciting, novel pursuit, leaving a wake of unfinished endeavors.
- **Difficulty Shifting Gears**: Once you do start, it can be hard to stop or transition to another task, especially if you're hyper focused on something. Paradoxically, while starting is hard, stopping can be just as difficult. When the ADHD brain latches onto something deeply engaging, it can enter a state of "hyperfocus," where attention becomes intensely concentrated, making it challenging to disengage and transition to other necessary tasks, even important ones. This can lead to imbalances, where one area of life receives disproportionate attention while others are neglected.
- **Underestimating the "Small Steps"**: Overlooking the power of tiny actions, leading to the belief that you need a huge burst of motivation to begin. There's a misconception that starting a large task requires an equally large amount of motivation. This leads to waiting for the "perfect" moment or a surge of energy that rarely arrives. The reality for ADHD is that motivation often *follows* action, rather than preceding it. The idea of breaking down tasks into almost trivially small steps is often dismissed as too simple, yet it's profoundly effective in overcoming inertia.

These challenges aren't a sign of laziness; they're a direct consequence of how the ADHD brain processes motivation, reward, and executive signals. The neurological pathways involved in dopamine regulation, which are critical for motivation and reward, function differently. This means that tasks that lack immediate, intrinsic interest or a clear, immediate reward can be extraordinarily difficult to initiate and sustain. The good news is that just like any skill, task initiation and follow-through can be strengthened with the right strategies, creating external structures and mental habits that provide the necessary activation energy and sustained momentum.

Breaking the Inertia: Strategies for Task Initiation

Getting started is often the hardest part. The key is to reduce the perceived effort of beginning. This involves tricking your brain into starting by making the initial step so small or so appealing that the resistance diminishes. The goal is to lower the "activation energy" required for your executive functions to kick in. Once momentum builds, the subsequent steps often become easier, as the brain's reward system begins to engage with the progress being made.

The 5-Minute Rule:

If a task seems daunting, commit to working on it for just five minutes. Tell yourself, "I just need to do this for five minutes." Often, once you start, the inertia breaks, and you'll find yourself continuing far beyond that initial five minutes. If not, you've still made a start, and that's a win. This strategy leverages the psychological principle of momentum. The most difficult part of any task is typically the very beginning. By committing to a ridiculously small amount of time, you bypass the brain's natural resistance to large, overwhelming tasks.

Five minutes feels manageable, even for the most dreaded chore or project. More often than not, once those five minutes are up, the task isn't as bad as you thought, or you've already made enough progress to feel motivated to continue. Even if you stop after five minutes, you've still achieved something, reducing the guilt of full procrastination and building a small but important habit of initiation.

Make the First Step Obvious and Tiny:

Don't think about "writing the report." Think about "opening the document" or "typing the title." For a chore, don't think "clean the kitchen," think "put one dish in the sink." Break the task down until the first action is so small it feels almost ridiculous not to do it. This is about clarifying the *very first physical action* required. Vague tasks such as "study for exam" are overwhelming. "Open textbook to Chapter 3" is a concrete, tiny step. "Exercise" is daunting; "put on running shoes" is a tiny, non-threatening step. The smaller and more explicit the first step, the less mental resistance your brain will encounter. This technique is particularly potent when combined with externalizing your plans.

Writing down that tiny first step can make it feel like a directive you simply have to follow. This bypasses the need for a huge burst of motivation and focuses on the power of micro-actions.

Use an "Action Hook":

Pair a new, difficult task with an established habit. For example, "After I pour my coffee, I will open my planner to review my top three tasks." Or "When I finish lunch, I'll spend 10 minutes on that project." This strategy, often discussed in habit formation, is incredibly effective for task initiation in ADHD. By linking a new, desired behavior (initiating a difficult task) to an existing, automatic habit, you create a "hook" that pulls you into action. Your brain already has a strong neural pathway for the established habit; by attaching a new action to it, you leverage that existing momentum. The key is consistency in the pairing. Over time, the new action will become more automatic, reducing the effort required for initiation. Identify habits you perform daily without thinking (e.g., brushing teeth, checking phone, eating breakfast) and consciously attach a small, desired task to them.

Remove Obstacles:

Clear your workspace. Gather all necessary materials before you start. If you need to make a call, have the number ready. The fewer barriers between you and the task, the easier it is to initiate. Think of this as clearing the runway for takeoff. Any small obstacle, whether physical (a messy desk) or logistical (missing a necessary document or tool), can provide an excuse for the ADHD brain to defer initiation. By proactively setting up your environment for success, you minimize friction. This includes preparing your digital workspace (closing unnecessary tabs, organizing files), ensuring you have all physical supplies, and anticipating any information you might need. The less "setup" a task requires in the moment, the smoother the transition from intention to action. This also reduces decision fatigue, as choices about "what to do next" have already been made.

Gamify It:

Turn tasks into a game. Set a timer, compete with yourself, or use apps that track your progress and reward you for starting. Even small, internal rewards can kick start motivation. The ADHD brain often responds well to novelty, challenge, and immediate feedback. Gamification taps into this. Set a timer for 25 minutes (Pomodoro Technique) and challenge yourself to focus for the entire duration. Use an app that tracks your completed tasks and provides virtual rewards or points. Compete with your past self to beat a certain time limit. The element of play can transform a dreaded chore into a stimulating challenge, leveraging your brain's natural inclination towards engaging activities and providing the intermittent bursts of dopamine that aid in motivation and sustained effort.

"Body Doubling":

Work alongside someone else, even if they're doing something completely different. The mere presence of another person can provide a subtle accountability and energy that helps initiate and sustain focus. This can be in person, via video call, or even in a co-working space.

This is a remarkably effective strategy for many with ADHD. The external presence of another person, even if they are silent and working on their own tasks, provides a gentle, non-judgmental form of accountability. It can create a subtle pressure to stay on task and can reduce feelings of isolation that sometimes accompany solo work. The other person acts as an external executive function, providing a stable, non-distracting presence that helps to anchor your attention and initiate action.

Many online communities now offer virtual body doubling sessions, making this accessible even if you don't have someone physically nearby.

Change Your Environment:

If you're stuck, sometimes simply moving to a different room, a coffee shop, or even just shifting your chair can break the mental block and signal to your brain that it's time to start something new. A change of scenery can provide a powerful cognitive reset. If you're struggling to start a task at your desk, try moving to a different table, a quiet corner, or even a different building. The novelty of the new environment can provide a subtle boost to attention and break the mental association with procrastination in your usual workspace. Even smaller changes, like standing up, stretching, or simply moving your laptop to a different part of the desk, can be enough to signal a fresh start to your brain and help break the inertia.

The Long Haul: Strategies for Follow-Through

Starting is great, but finishing is where the real impact happens. Maintaining momentum is key. The initial excitement of a new project often provides enough dopamine to get you going. However, as the novelty wears off and the grind sets in, maintaining focus and persistence becomes significantly harder for the ADHD brain. This is where strategic reinforcement and intentional motivation come into play, designed to bridge the gap between initial enthusiasm and sustained effort, preventing the dreaded "half-finished" pile.

Visualize the End Goal:

Before and during a task, take a moment to clearly picture the finished product or the positive outcome of completing it. How will it feel? What benefits will it bring? This extrinsic motivation can be powerful for the ADHD brain. When tasks become tedious, the intrinsic reward often diminishes. By consistently visualizing the positive outcome, you provide your brain with a tangible "future reward" that can help bridge the motivational gap. If you're working on a difficult report, imagine the relief and satisfaction of submitting it, or the positive feedback you'll receive. If you're cleaning, picture the calm and order of a tidy space. This mental rehearsal provides a continuous source of positive reinforcement, reminding your brain *why* the sustained effort is worthwhile.

Regular Check-Ins (and Rewards):

Don't wait until the end to acknowledge progress. Break down large tasks into smaller milestones and build in mini-rewards for completing each one. This could be a 5-minute break, a favorite song, or a quick walk. The ADHD brain thrives on immediate feedback and rewards. Large, long-term goals often lack the continuous positive reinforcement needed to sustain attention. By breaking tasks into smaller, more digestible milestones, you create more opportunities for "wins." Each completed milestone can be celebrated with a small, immediate reward. This doesn't have to be anything grand – simply standing up and stretching, listening to one song, or allowing yourself a few minutes of guilt-free Browse. These mini-rewards provide regular dopamine boosts, reinforcing the behavior of following through and making the long haul feel less arduous.

Combat the "Novelty Effect":

The ADHD brain thrives on newness. When a task starts to feel routine or boring, try to inject novelty. Can you do it in a different order? Use a new tool? Listen to different music? Change your environment mid-task? This strategy directly addresses the ADHD brain's hunger for novelty. When a task loses its initial spark, consciously look for ways to make it fresh again. If you're writing, try using a different font or a different writing app. If you're working on data entry, try doing it in a different room or listening to a different genre of music. Even small changes can re-engage your attention and provide a temporary boost of interest, helping you push through the "boring" parts of a long task. This is about creative problem-solving to maintain engagement, rather than waiting for motivation to magically reappear.

Accountability Partners:

Share your goals and progress with a trusted friend, family member, or colleague. Knowing someone else is aware of your commitments can provide a powerful external motivator to follow through. External accountability can be a game-changer for follow-through. When you've publicly stated a goal, there's a natural desire to follow through to maintain your credibility or avoid disappointing someone. This provides an external structure that compensates for internal motivational dips. Choose someone supportive, who understands ADHD, and establish clear expectations for check-ins (e.g., daily text message updates, weekly calls). The simple act of knowing someone will ask about your progress can be enough to push you through moments of resistance.

"Future Self" Letter:

Write a short note to your future self, reminding yourself why this task is important and the positive feelings associated with its completion. Read it when motivation wanes. This technique leverages the power of self-empathy and foresight. When you're in the midst of a tedious task, it's easy to lose sight of the bigger picture. By writing a letter to your "future self" when you're feeling motivated, you create a tangible reminder of the positive outcomes and the "why" behind your efforts. When you hit a wall, reading this letter can re-connect you to your initial intention and provide a much-needed emotional and motivational boost, helping you push through to completion.

Automate and Systemize:

Wherever possible, create systems that reduce the need for conscious effort in follow-through. Set recurring reminders, use templates, or automate routine steps. The less you have to think about it, the more likely you are to do it. The ADHD brain thrives on automation and consistent systems because they reduce decision fatigue and the reliance on inconsistent executive functions. Set up recurring calendar reminders for tasks that need to be done regularly. Use email templates for common responses. Create checklists for multi-step processes. Automate bill payments. The goal is to offload as much routine cognitive load as possible, freeing up your mental energy for tasks that truly require your focused attention and creativity. Systems create predictability and consistency, making follow-through less about willpower and more about habit.

Embrace Imperfection:

The desire for perfection can be a huge blocker to follow-through. Remind yourself that "done is better than perfect." The goal is completion, not flawlessness, especially in the initial stages. Perfectionism is a common, yet often unrecognized, form of procrastination for men with ADHD. The fear of not doing something perfectly can prevent you from starting or, more commonly, from finishing. The ADHD brain can get bogged down in details, endlessly tweaking and refining, leading to unfinished projects. Consciously remind yourself that "perfect is the enemy of good." The goal is to get the task *done* to an acceptable standard, then move on. You can always revisit and refine later if truly necessary. Prioritize completion over unattainable perfection, and watch your pile of half-finished projects shrink.

Cultivating robust task initiation and follow-through means developing a consistent bridge between your intentions and your actions. It's about building momentum and learning to ride that wave, even when it feels like the current is pulling you in another direction. By implementing these strategies, you'll transform your ability to not only start but also complete tasks, moving from a cycle of good intentions to one of consistent accomplishment. This mastery provides a profound sense of control and competence, allowing you to reliably translate your ideas and aspirations into concrete realities, paving the way for sustained success and reduced stress in all areas of your life.

CHAPTER 5:

DEVELOPING SELF-REGULATION AND IMPULSE CONTROL

At the very core of your executive function command center lies the critical ability to self-regulate and control impulses. Think of these as your brain's internal brakes and steering wheel, allowing you to pause, think, and choose a deliberate response rather than simply reacting to every urge, emotion, or distraction. While planning and initiation help you start and guide your journey, self-regulation and impulse control ensure you stay on course, avoid collisions, and reach your destination safely and efficiently. These are not merely optional skills but fundamental capacities that dictate your ability to navigate complex social situations, manage personal finances, maintain professional decorum, and pursue long-term goals without being constantly derailed by immediate gratification or emotional surges. For men with ADHD, the development of these capacities is not about eliminating the unique energetic and responsive nature of your brain, but rather about channelling it with greater intentionality and purpose. It's about empowering you to direct your inner force, rather than being swept away by it.

For men with ADHD, the internal brakes can sometimes feel a bit spongy, and the steering wheel might occasionally get a mind of its own. This isn't a moral failing; it's a neurological difference that often manifests as a disjunction between intention and action, particularly when faced with a strong immediate stimulus or emotion. The underlying neurobiology of ADHD, involving variations in the function of the prefrontal cortex and the regulation of neurotransmitters like dopamine and norepinephrine, means that the brain's "stop" signals and its ability to delay gratification are less robust. This translates into a heightened sensitivity to immediate rewards and a reduced capacity to inhibit automatic responses, even when those responses are counterproductive to long-term goals or positive relationships. This foundational difference contributes to common challenges such as:

- **Difficulty managing emotions**: Intense frustration, anger, or excitement can lead to outbursts or withdrawal, without a pause for thoughtful response. For men with ADHD, emotions can often feel amplified and rapidly shifting. A minor inconvenience might trigger a disproportionate burst of anger, or perceived criticism could send you into a spiral of intense shame or despair (often linked to Rejection Sensitive Dysphoria, as discussed in Book 4). The "lag time" between feeling an intense emotion and acting on it is significantly shorter, leading to regrettable words or actions that can strain personal and professional relationships. The challenge isn't the emotion itself, but the lack of an effective internal buffer to process it before reacting.

- **Impulsive spending**: Acting on a sudden desire to buy something, leading to financial strain or regret. The allure of immediate gratification, coupled with a reduced ability to foresee long-term consequences, can make impulsive purchases a significant challenge. Whether it's a new gadget, an expensive meal, or an online shopping spree, these decisions are often made in the moment, driven by a desire for a quick dopamine hit, only to be followed by financial stress and regret.

- **Interrupting conversations**: The thought feels so urgent, it bursts out before you can process politeness or turn-taking. This often stems from a rapid flow of ideas and a difficulty inhibiting the urge to express them immediately. While not intended as rude, frequent interruptions can make others feel unheard, devalued, or frustrated, impacting social connections and professional interactions. The internal experience is one of a thought feeling so critical that if not expressed immediately, it will be lost forever.
- **Jumping to conclusions**: Reacting to incomplete information without taking time to gather all the facts. The ADHD brain's tendency to process information quickly and sometimes superficially, combined with a difficulty inhibiting initial interpretations, can lead to hasty judgments. This can result in misunderstandings, miscommunications, and reactive behaviors based on partial or inaccurate information, particularly in emotionally charged situations.
- **Struggling with gratification delay**: Choosing immediate, smaller rewards over larger, long-term benefits (e.g., scrolling social media instead of working on a crucial project). The "now" bias is strong in ADHD. The brain is wired to prioritize immediate pleasure or relief from discomfort, making it exceptionally difficult to defer satisfaction for a more significant, but distant, reward. This directly impacts long-term goal achievement, health habits, and financial planning.
- **Addictive behaviors**: A heightened susceptibility to developing habits around things that provide immediate dopamine hits, from gaming to unhealthy food. The brain's search for stimulation and reward, combined with challenges in self-control, can make individuals with ADHD more vulnerable to developing habits that provide quick dopamine boosts, whether through excessive screen time, substance use, or other compulsive behaviors. These behaviors can become self-perpetuating, offering temporary relief from internal discomfort but ultimately undermining overall well-being.

These challenges can impact every facet of life, from professional reputation to personal relationships and overall well-being. The good news is that just like strengthening a muscle, you can train your brain to improve its capacity for self-regulation and impulse control. This training involves a combination of environmental adjustments, cognitive restructuring, and behavioral practices that create a more robust internal regulatory system. It's about building a conscious buffer between stimulus and response, allowing you to make intentional choices that align with your long-term values and goals, rather than being driven by fleeting urges or intense emotions.

Hitting the Brakes: Strategies for Impulse Control

The first step in controlling impulses is creating a pause – a small window between stimulus and response. This pause is where the power of choice resides. Without it, your actions are automatic reactions. For the ADHD brain, this pause is often short or non-existent, making intentional intervention crucial. By consciously inserting this moment, you gain the opportunity to engage your executive functions – to think, plan, and then act deliberately.

The "Stop, Think, Act" Method:

This is a foundational strategy. When you feel an impulse arising (to interrupt, to buy something, to lash out), physically **STOP** what you're doing. Take a deep breath. **THINK**: What is the consequence of this action? What is my goal right now? What are alternative responses? Then, **ACT** deliberately. This simple, three-step process is a powerful circuit breaker for impulsivity. The "STOP" doesn't just mean a mental pause; it often benefits from a *physical* stop. Put down what you're holding, take a step back, or even clench your fist and release it. This physical interruption helps to disengage the automatic, reactive pathways in your brain. The "THINK" phase is where you engage your prefrontal cortex, asking questions that force a consideration of consequences and alternatives.

For example, if you feel an urge to angrily reply to an email, the "THINK" step involves considering: "If I send this now, how will it impact my professional relationship? Is there a more constructive way to communicate my point?" Only after this deliberate thought process do you "ACT" with intention, choosing a response that aligns with your desired outcome. Consistent practice with this method gradually extends the pause, making deliberate action more accessible.

Delay Gratification with a Timer:

If you have an impulse to do something distracting or less productive (e.g., check social media, eat a snack), set a timer for 10-15 minutes. Tell yourself, "I can do this, but not right now." Often, the urge will pass or diminish in that time. This strategy directly targets the "now" bias inherent in ADHD. The brain desires immediate reward or relief from discomfort. By setting a timer, you acknowledge the urge ("Yes, I want to check social media"), but you defer the gratification. This simple act trains your brain to tolerate discomfort and delay reward. You're teaching it that the reward *will* come, just not instantly. In many cases, by the time the timer goes off, the intensity of the urge has significantly decreased, or you've become re-engaged in your productive task. Start with short delays and gradually increase them as your capacity for gratification delay improves.

Physical Barriers:

Make impulsive actions harder to do. If you impulsively buy online, delete saved credit card details or unsubscribe from tempting retail emails. If you interrupt, try putting a hand over your mouth or biting your tongue gently (without hurting yourself!) to create a physical reminder to pause. This is about creating "friction" between the impulse and the action. By making impulsive behaviors more difficult or inconvenient, you give your executive functions a chance to intervene. For online shopping, moving credit cards to a harder-to-reach location, unsubscribing from marketing emails, or even using a browser extension that forces a "cooling-off" period before purchase can be effective. In conversations, a subtle physical cue like gently pressing your tongue to the roof of your mouth, or lightly gripping your hands under the table, can serve as a non-verbal "stop" signal, allowing you to pause before an interruption slips out. The goal is to build an external or physical "speed bump" for your impulses.

"Think It Through" Questions:

Before making a quick decision, especially a significant one, ask yourself:

- "Is this truly necessary right now?"
- "What are the immediate and long-term consequences?"
- "Is there a better way to address this?"
- "Am I feeling a strong emotion that's influencing this decision?" These questions serve as a mental checklist, forcing a more comprehensive and rational evaluation of an impulse before acting. The ADHD brain often operates on "fast-thinking" (System 1 thinking), relying on intuition and immediate emotional responses. These questions encourage "slow-thinking" (System 2 thinking), which is more analytical and deliberate. By consciously asking about necessity, consequences, alternatives, and emotional influence, you engage the prefrontal cortex, providing an opportunity for wiser decision-making. This is particularly helpful for major financial decisions, significant relationship discussions, or high-stakes professional interactions where impulsive actions can have lasting negative repercussions.

Identify Triggers:

Become aware of what situations, emotions, or thoughts tend to precede your impulsive behaviors. Is it stress? Boredom? Certain people? Once you identify your triggers, you can develop proactive strategies to avoid or navigate them. Impulse control is often about proactive prevention rather than reactive suppression. By diligently observing and logging your impulsive behaviors, you can start to discern patterns. Do you tend to interrupt more when you're tired, or when a specific topic comes up? Do you overspend when you're feeling stressed or bored? Once identified, triggers become points of intervention. You can then create an "If-Then" plan for each: "IF I feel bored during a meeting, THEN I will doodle notes instead of checking my phone." Or "IF I feel stressed, THEN I will take a 5-minute walk before opening any online shopping sites." This moves you from a reactive stance to a proactive one.

Scheduled "Impulse Releases":

Sometimes the urge to do something (like check your phone) is overwhelming. Instead of constantly fighting it, schedule specific short "release" times throughout your day where you allow yourself to indulge in those impulses for a brief period. This can reduce the constant mental battle. This strategy acknowledges the ADHD brain's powerful need for novelty and stimulation. Trying to suppress all impulses for an extended period can lead to intense mental fatigue and eventual relapse. Instead, create controlled "release valves." For example, if you know you have an urge to check social media every 30 minutes, schedule a 5-minute social media break every hour. This gives your brain permission to look forward to the "reward" and reduces the need to constantly fight against the urge. It turns an unconscious, disruptive behavior into a conscious, managed one, allowing for greater focus during your designated work periods.

Guiding the Wheel: Strategies for Self-Regulation

Self-regulation extends beyond impulse control; it's about consciously managing your states – your energy, your focus, and your emotions – to align with your goals. It's the overarching ability to monitor and adjust your thoughts, feelings, and behaviors to achieve desired outcomes, particularly in the face of challenging situations or tempting distractions. For men with ADHD, cultivating robust self-regulation means building a flexible internal steering mechanism that can navigate the unpredictable terrain of daily life, keeping you aligned with your values and long-term aspirations. It's about developing an internal compass that guides you back on track when you drift, not just slamming on the brakes when you're about to crash.

Mindfulness and Body Scans:

Regularly check in with your body and mind. What are you feeling? Where is tension? Is your mind racing? Simple mindfulness exercises (e.g., focusing on your breath for one minute) can create a mental space to observe your internal state without immediately reacting to it. This awareness is the foundation of self-regulation. Mindfulness trains your attention to the present moment, which is a key skill for self-regulation. For the ADHD brain, which often operates at high speed or drifts into past regrets/future worries, mindfulness provides an anchor. A quick body scan – mentally checking in with sensations in different parts of your body – can ground you and reveal underlying tension or emotional states you weren't consciously aware of. This increased interoception (awareness of internal bodily states) helps you recognize emotional arousal *before* it escalates, providing a crucial window for intervention. Regular short mindfulness practices (2-5 minutes daily) build this foundational awareness, making you more attuned to your internal landscape.

Emotional Labeling:

When strong emotions arise, try to identify and name them: "I'm feeling intense frustration right now." "This is anger." Labeling emotions helps to distance yourself from them slightly, giving you a chance to respond thoughtfully rather than being swept away. Research in affect labeling shows that simply putting a name to an emotion can reduce its intensity by activating the prefrontal cortex and dampening the amygdala's response. For men with ADHD, who may experience emotions with greater intensity and less processing time, this is incredibly powerful. Instead of just feeling "bad" or "overwhelmed," explicitly identifying "This is sadness," or "This is anxiety," creates a small but significant cognitive distance from the emotion. This distance allows for a more rational assessment and prevents being completely consumed by the feeling, opening the door for a more measured response.

The "Zone of Regulation" Check-in:

Learn to recognize your emotional zones (e.g., Green Zone: calm, focused; Yellow Zone: anxious, agitated; Red Zone: angry, out of control). Develop a toolkit of strategies for each zone to help you return to the Green. For Yellow, it might be taking a walk; for Red, it might be deep breathing or stepping away. This framework, often used in emotional education, helps you categorize and proactively manage your emotional state. Instead of waiting for an emotional crisis, you learn to identify early warning signs (Yellow Zone) and apply preventative strategies. This might involve a personalized list of "calming tools" for the Yellow Zone (e.g., listening to music, talking to a trusted friend, doing a quick chore) and "crisis tools" for the Red Zone (e.g., intense exercise, splashing cold water on your face). Regularly checking in with your "zone" allows for continuous, proactive emotional steering.

Strategic Breaks and Movement:

Your brain needs regular resets. Short, intentional breaks (5-10 minutes) can prevent emotional build-up and mental fatigue. Physical movement, even just stretching or walking around, can significantly aid in self-regulation by discharging excess energy and helping you reset your focus. The ADHD brain is not built for sustained, static effort. Movement is a natural regulator of dopamine and norepinephrine, helping to manage restlessness and improve cognitive function.

Strategic breaks, beyond just Pomodoro-style work breaks, are essential for emotional well-being. This might involve stepping outside for a few minutes, doing some push-ups or jumping jacks, or even just dancing to a favorite song. These "brain breaks" prevent cognitive and emotional overload, allowing you to return to your tasks with renewed focus and emotional equilibrium.

Prepare for High-Stimulus Environments:

If you know you're going into a situation that triggers impulsivity or overstimulation (e.g., a noisy meeting, a crowded store), have a plan. This might involve setting a time limit, wearing noise-canceling headphones, or having an exit strategy. Anticipation is a powerful self-regulation tool. For men with ADHD, certain environments can be highly dysregulating, leading to overwhelm, irritability, or impulsive actions. By pre-planning how to navigate these situations, you reduce the in-the-moment cognitive load. This might mean deciding in advance to only stay at a crowded event for a set amount of time, bringing noise-canceling headphones to a busy office, or having pre-scripted phrases to politely exit a conversation if you feel overwhelmed. This proactive approach reduces the likelihood of an emotional or behavioral derailment.

Practice Self-Compassion:

Developing self-regulation is a journey, not a destination. You will make mistakes. Instead of dwelling on them, practice self-compassion. Acknowledge the misstep, learn from it, and recommit to your strategies. Harsh self-criticism only depletes the emotional resources needed for regulation. For men with ADHD, who often carry a lifetime of perceived failures or criticisms, the inner critic can be particularly damaging. Self-compassion is not self-indulgence; it's a powerful motivator.

When you inevitably stumble, treating yourself with kindness and understanding (as you would a good friend) helps you recover faster, learn from the experience, and re-engage with your strategies. Harsh self-criticism triggers shame and anxiety, which further undermine self-regulation. By fostering an inner ally, you build emotional resilience and create a supportive internal environment for growth.

By diligently practicing these strategies, you'll find yourself increasingly capable of pausing before reacting, making more intentional choices, and navigating your emotional landscape with greater control. Developing self-regulation and impulse control is not about suppressing who you are, but about empowering you to direct your energy and attention towards the life you genuinely want to build. It's the ultimate command over your own brain's operations, transforming inherent challenges into cultivated strengths, allowing you to live with greater purpose, peace, and sustained effectiveness.

CONCLUSION:
YOUR SHARPENED MIND

You've reached the end of Book 1, and in doing so, you've taken a significant step toward understanding and strengthening the very core of your cognitive abilities: your **executive functions**. These functions are largely managed by the prefrontal cortex, which, as we touched on in Chapter 1, shows different activity patterns and neurotransmitter regulation in individuals with ADHD. For example, challenges in **response inhibition** (the ability to stop or hold back impulses) are directly linked to these neurobiological differences, often contributing to impulsivity in thought, speech, and action.

We've journeyed through the intricacies of your brain's command center, acknowledging the unique ways ADHD impacts these crucial skills, not as deficits, but as areas ripe for strategic cultivation.

From enhancing your **working memory** and focusing your **attention**, to mastering the art of **planning and prioritization**, and finally, cultivating resilient **task initiation and follow-through** alongside powerful **self-regulation and impulse control**, you've gained invaluable insights and practical strategies.

This book isn't just about theory; it's about equipping you with actionable tools to reclaim control over your daily life. You've learned to:

- **Externalize and visualize** information to bolster your memory.
- **Create "attention zones"** and use techniques like Pomodoro to sharpen your focus.
- **Break down daunting tasks** and prioritize effectively with frameworks like the Eisenhower Matrix.
- **Overcome inertia** with the 5-Minute Rule and build consistent follow-through.
- **Pause and choose** your responses more deliberately, managing impulses and emotions.

Remember, the journey of strengthening your executive functions is an ongoing process. There will be days when the strategies click into place effortlessly, and days when the old patterns re-emerge. This is normal. The key is **consistency**, **self-compassion**, and a willingness to **adapt** what you've learned to suit your unique neurobiology.

The foundation you've built in this book is crucial. You now have a deeper understanding of *how* your brain works and *what* you can do to support its optimal performance. This sharpened mind isn't about eradicating ADHD; it's about empowering you to leverage your strengths, navigate challenges with greater ease, and ultimately, live a more intentional and fulfilling life.

As you move forward, carry these tools with you. Practice them daily. Observe what works best for *you*. With each conscious effort, you're not just managing ADHD; you're actively shaping a more responsive, resilient, and effective version of yourself.

Let's pause for a moment and reflect on what you've just read. What resonates with you? What are the strategies you feel you can apply to work and life now versus those that seem more challenging or daunting?

BOOK TWO:
MASTERING FOCUS:
SUSTAINED ATTENTION IN A DISTRACTING WORLD

CHAPTER 1:

UNDERSTANDING THE ADHD FOCUS CHALLENGE

In Book 1, we explored your brain's command center and its executive functions, laying the groundwork for better self-management. We established that executive functions are the sophisticated managers of your mind, guiding you through planning, task initiation, and self-regulation. Now, we're going to dive deeper into one of the most persistent and often misunderstood aspects of ADHD: focus. It's not just about paying attention; it's about sustained attention: the ability to maintain your mental spotlight on a task or thought for an extended period, especially when there are countless other things vying for that light. This capacity for sustained, directed attention is the bedrock upon which productivity, deep learning, and meaningful engagement are built.

For individuals with ADHD, this bedrock often feels less like solid ground and more like shifting sand, presenting a unique and often frustrating challenge that impacts every facet of daily life. The distinction between merely "paying attention" and "sustaining attention" is critical; the former is a fleeting moment, while the latter is an enduring state, a continuous act of conscious mental direction.

For many men with ADHD, the concept of "focus" can feel like a cruel paradox. On one hand, you might experience intense periods of hyperfocus, where you become completely engrossed in a task or interest, often to the exclusion of everything else—food, sleep, or urgent responsibilities. This state, while sometimes incredibly productive for specific, engaging tasks, is often uncontrolled and can lead to imbalances, such as neglecting critical deadlines for a captivating new hobby. On the other hand, for tasks that lack immediate novelty, stimulation, or personal interest, maintaining focus can feel like trying to catch smoke with your bare hands. Your attention flits, jumps, and scatters, leaving you feeling frustrated and unproductive. This isn't a deliberate choice or a sign of laziness; it is an inherent characteristic of how your brain processes and prioritizes stimuli.

The mental effort required to maintain attention on a mundane task can be immense, leading to rapid cognitive fatigue and the constant allure of more stimulating alternatives. This constant battle for sustained attention creates a pervasive sense of internal struggle, leading to feelings of inadequacy and a cyclical pattern of starting and abandoning tasks.

This isn't a lack of desire or willpower; it's a fundamental difference in how your brain regulates attention. While a neurotypical brain might act like a sophisticated filter, effortlessly tuning out irrelevant stimuli, the ADHD brain often struggles with this inhibition. This challenge stems from differences in neurochemistry, particularly in the pathways involving dopamine and norepinephrine, which are vital for motivation, reward, and attention.

Dopamine, often called the "feel-good" neurotransmitter, is crucial for regulating the brain's reward system, motivation, and the ability to find tasks interesting enough to sustain focus. In ADHD, there's often a dysregulation in how dopamine is transported and utilized, leading to a diminished baseline level of stimulation. This means that tasks that are inherently boring or effortful provide less intrinsic reward, making it harder to initiate and sustain engagement. Norepinephrine plays a key role in alertness and arousal; its dysregulation can impact the brain's ability to maintain an optimal state of readiness for focused work.

Also, variations in the activity of specific brain networks, such as the Default Mode Network (DMN), which is associated with mind-wandering and introspection, and the Task Positive Network (TPN), which is involved in focused, goal-directed attention, contribute to the difficulty in sustaining attention and inhibiting distractions. In the neurotypical brain, these networks operate in a kind of "seesaw" fashion: when one is active, the other is suppressed. In the ADHD brain, the DMN can remain overly active even when the TPN is supposed to be engaged, leading to intrusive thoughts and a struggle to stay "on task." This under-filtering of both internal and external stimuli means the ADHD brain is constantly bombarded, making it difficult to select and maintain focus on any single input.

The 'ADHD focus challenge' isn't a single issue, but a multifaceted one:

- **Distractibility:** Both external (a phone notification, a colleague walking by, a siren outside) and internal (a sudden memory, a new idea, a nagging worry about an upcoming task, a self-critical thought) stimuli can pull your attention off course with remarkable ease. For the ADHD brain, every piece of information, whether relevant or not, seems to register with almost equal weight. It's as if the brain's sensory gates are perpetually open, allowing a flood of data to enter, making it incredibly difficult to prioritize and filter. This leads to a constant internal "pinging" effect, where your attention is fragmented, leading to a pervasive sense of mental exhaustion. A quick glance at a notification can turn into 20 minutes lost down an internet rabbit hole, or a fleeting thought about what to cook for dinner can derail an hour of productive work. The challenge is not a lack of *ability* to focus, but a profound difficulty in *choosing* what to focus on and then *ignoring* everything else. This constant battle against stimuli is a significant drain on executive function.

- **Difficulty Shifting Focus:** While easy to distract, it can also be difficult to intentionally shift focus back to a less stimulating but important task once diverted, or even to transition from one task to another. This is often referred to as "attentional inertia" or "stickiness." Once the ADHD brain latches onto a new, stimulating input (a distraction or an engaging new project), it can be incredibly difficult to disengage from it. It's like a train that's hard to get started, but once it's moving, it's also hard to stop or switch tracks. This means that a brief distraction can lead to extended periods of being off-task. Similarly, transitioning between different types of tasks, even planned ones (e.g., from creative writing to administrative work), can be a significant hurdle, requiring a substantial amount of mental energy to "unstick" from one cognitive mode and initiate another. This contributes to the feeling of being "stuck" or paralyzed when attempting to move between items on a to-do list.

- **Inconsistent Focus (The "On/Off" Switch):** Your ability to focus might fluctuate wildly throughout the day, or even within an hour, often leaving you at the mercy of your brain's unpredictable shifts. Unlike a neurotypical individual who might experience a gradual dip in focus, the ADHD brain's focus can feel like an erratic light switch – either intensely on (hyperfocus) or completely off (scattered and unfocused), with little in-between. This inconsistency makes it incredibly difficult to plan reliable work blocks or predict your productivity. One day you might power through a complex task, and the next, the same task feels insurmountable. This unpredictability can lead to significant frustration, as you're constantly battling an internal state that seems outside your control. This also contributes to the "ADHD tax": the extra time, effort, and often financial cost incurred due to inconsistent performance, missed deadlines, or redoing work.

- **Under-stimulation vs. Overstimulation:** You might struggle to focus because a task is too boring (under-stimulating), leading to mind-wandering and a desperate search for internal or external novelty, or because your environment is too chaotic (overstimulating), leading to overwhelm and scattered attention. The ADHD brain is constantly seeking an optimal level of stimulation. If a task is not engaging enough (e.g., repetitive data entry, reading a dense policy document), the brain will actively seek out alternative, more stimulating internal or external stimuli, leading to boredom, restlessness, and mind-wandering. Conversely, if the environment is too rich with sensory input (e.g., open-plan office noise, multiple conversations, bright lights, cluttered space), the brain becomes overstimulated, leading to sensory overload, irritability, and an inability to filter out irrelevant information. Finding the "just right" level of stimulation is a constant balancing act for optimal focus, requiring careful environmental design and self-awareness.

- **"Time Blindness":** A poor internal sense of time can exacerbate focus issues, making it hard to accurately perceive the passage of time, estimate how long tasks will take, or understand the immediacy of future events. While not a formal diagnostic term, "time blindness" is a widely recognized and impactful experience for many with ADHD. This means that "soon" or "later" can feel like an abstract concept, and even short intervals can be misjudged. This contributes to chronic lateness, difficulty allocating appropriate attention to tasks (either underestimating or overestimating time needed), and a struggle to prioritize based on future deadlines. The future often feels less "real" than the immediate present, making it challenging to invest in long-term goals when immediate gratification or a pressing, last-minute demand beckons. This makes sustained, future-oriented focus particularly challenging, as the reward seems too distant to motivate consistent effort.

The impact of these challenges ripples through every aspect of life. Professionally, it can mean missed deadlines, incomplete projects, difficulty staying engaged in meetings (leading to perceptions of disinterest), or struggling with complex, multi-stage assignments. Your career progression might feel stalled, or you might find yourself consistently underperforming despite possessing high intelligence and capability. Personally, it can lead to miscommunications in relationships (e.g., forgetting details of conversations, not being present), forgotten chores, an inability to relax and be present with loved ones (as your mind races), or neglecting personal health goals.

The cumulative effect of these daily struggles is significant: it contributes to pervasive feelings of overwhelm, anxiety, and a deep-seated sense that you're constantly fighting your own brain. This internal battle often leads to self-criticism, shame, and a belief that you are simply not "good enough" or "disciplined enough," further eroding self-esteem and hindering your ability to engage effectively with strategies that could help. The mental load of managing these challenges is exhausting, leading to burnout and a cycle of underachievement relative to potential.

But here's the empowering truth: while your brain is wired differently, you can absolutely learn to exert greater influence over your attention. Mastering focus for the ADHD brain isn't about forcing yourself to conform to neurotypical norms; it's about understanding your unique cognitive landscape and implementing strategies that work *with* your brain's natural tendencies. It's about recognizing that your brain's unique wiring, while presenting challenges, also often comes with strengths like creativity, divergent thinking, high energy for novel tasks, and the capacity for intense hyperfocus when engaged. The goal is to harness these strengths and build compensatory systems and habits that mitigate the challenges. This involves strategic environmental design, internal cognitive shifts, and the consistent practice of new behaviors that gradually re-wire your brain's attentional pathways. It's a journey of self-discovery and tailored optimization, recognizing that a "one-size-fits-all" approach to focus will likely fail.

In the chapters to come, we'll delve into practical, actionable strategies specifically designed for the ADHD brain's unique attentional patterns. We'll explore how to design your environment for optimal concentration by minimizing distractions and curating sensory input. We'll learn to harness the power of mindfulness to anchor your attention in the present moment, building greater self-awareness and control over your internal landscape. You'll discover how to master single-tasking and cultivate periods of deep work, leveraging techniques that reduce context switching and honor your brain's preference for focused engagement. Furthermore, we'll address strategies to build resilience to sustain focus without burning out, incorporating self-compassion and realistic expectations into your approach. This isn't about becoming a robot, devoid of your unique spontaneity and creativity; it's about empowering you to direct your mental energy where you want it to go, when you need it to go there. Get ready to transform your relationship with focus and unlock a powerful new edge in navigating a distracting world, allowing your inherent strengths to shine through with greater clarity and purpose.

CHAPTER 2:

ENVIRONMENTAL DESIGN FOR FOCUS

You now have a clearer understanding of how your ADHD brain approaches focus. We've seen that focus isn't a singular, monolithic skill, but a complex interplay of attention regulation, impulse control, and the brain's unique wiring regarding stimulation and reward. The good news is that while your internal landscape might be unique, you have significant control over your external environment. Just as a pilot checks their instruments and clears the runway before take-off, designing your surroundings can dramatically reduce distractions and prime your brain for sustained attention. This isn't about imposing rigid, uncomfortable rules, but rather about creating a supportive ecosystem for your brain, a space that minimizes friction and maximizes your capacity for deep, meaningful work. Think of it as creating a personalized, high-performance cockpit for your mind, tailored to its specific needs.

For men with ADHD, the environment isn't just a backdrop; it's an active participant in your ability to focus. A cluttered desk, a noisy office, a constantly vibrating phone, or even a strong visual stimulus from a window can be insurmountable barriers to deep work. Your brain is highly sensitive to external stimuli, and every unexpected sound, fleeting movement, or visual distraction acts like a siren call, pulling your mental spotlight away from your intended target. This isn't a sign of weakness, but a characteristic of the ADHD brain's reduced ability to filter out irrelevant information. While a neurotypical brain might effortlessly tune out the hum of the refrigerator or the distant chatter of colleagues, the ADHD brain registers these inputs with near-equal importance, demanding cognitive resources that could otherwise be directed towards your task. This constant barrage of competing stimuli leads to mental fatigue, frustration, and a diminished capacity for sustained attention.

The goal of environmental design isn't to create a sterile, silent chamber (unless that works for you!), but to consciously curate a space that supports your specific needs for concentration. It's about reducing friction, minimizing tempting distractions, and creating cues that signal "this is where I focus." This personalized approach recognizes that what's distracting for one person might be a helpful background for another. The aim is to proactively sculpt your surroundings to work *with* your brain's unique tendencies, rather than constantly fighting against them. This involves an iterative process of observation, experimentation, and adjustment, identifying what truly helps you achieve and maintain your desired state of focus. It's about taking command of your external world to empower your internal one.

Crafting Your "Attention Zone": Physical Space Strategies

Your physical workspace plays a monumental role in your ability to concentrate. Small, intentional changes can yield significant returns, transforming a chaotic environment into a sanctuary for focus. This isn't necessarily about having a dedicated home office, but rather about optimizing whatever space you have to create a distinct "attention zone" that cues your brain for productive work.

Declutter Ruthlessly:

A cluttered environment leads to a cluttered mind. Clear your desk or workspace of everything not directly related to your current task. For paperwork, use simple filing systems; for objects, give them a designated "home." The less visual noise, the easier it is for your brain to zero in on what matters. Visual clutter is a significant source of distraction for the ADHD brain. Each item on your desk or in your line of sight is a potential mental "ping," demanding a fraction of your attention. By ruthlessly decluttering, you reduce the number of competing stimuli, making it easier for your visual attention to settle on your work. This isn't about achieving a minimalist aesthetic, but about creating functional order. Implement a "one-touch" rule: if you pick something up, either put it away immediately, or take the next action on it. Regularly schedule 5-minute "micro-decluttering" sessions to prevent accumulation. Consider having only the essential tools for your *current* task on your desk, with everything else stored away in drawers or dedicated organizers. This practice frees up cognitive bandwidth by reducing the constant visual scanning and mental processing required to filter out irrelevant items.

Optimize for Your Senses:

Your sensory environment profoundly impacts your ability to focus. Tailoring it to your unique needs is critical.

- **Sound:** Experiment with sound. Some thrive in complete silence, others benefit from noise-cancelling headphones or ambient noise (e.g., white noise, nature sounds, classical music without lyrics). Find what helps you concentrate and consistently use it. For some, silence can be too under-stimulating, leading to internal distractions. For others, even minimal background noise is a significant interruption. Experiment: try a white noise generator, binaural beats, or instrumental music. Avoid music with lyrics if you find yourself getting distracted by them. Noise-cancelling headphones can create a powerful personal sound bubble in an otherwise noisy environment, signaling to your brain that it's time to focus. Consistently using your chosen sound environment helps build a habit, acting as an auditory cue for focus.
- **Sight:** Position your desk facing a wall, or in a way that minimizes foot traffic or windows with busy views. If you have a highly visual brain, even a picture frame on your desk can be a distraction. Use desk partitions or visual barriers if needed.

Visual distractions are potent attention hijackers for the ADHD brain. A busy hallway, a window overlooking an active street, or even a lively office environment can constantly pull your gaze and mind away from your work. If possible, arrange your workspace to minimize these visual inputs. If you can't reorient your desk, consider a small, portable partition or even strategically placed plants to block distracting lines of sight. For highly sensitive individuals, even personal decor items can be distracting; opt for a clean, visually calm workspace during focused periods.

- **Lighting:** Ensure adequate, natural light if possible. Poor lighting can cause eye strain and fatigue, making focus harder. Avoid harsh overhead lights that can be distracting. Natural light is generally beneficial for mood and alertness, supporting sustained focus. Position your workspace near a window, if possible, but be mindful of glare. If natural light isn't available, use warm, diffused lighting that mimics natural light and minimizes shadows or harsh glares. Task lighting (e.g., a desk lamp) can help illuminate your immediate work area without overstimulating the entire space. Avoid fluorescent lights, which can cause eye strain and be audibly distracting to some.
- **Comfort:** An uncomfortable chair, a too-hot or too-cold room, or even restrictive clothing can be constant, low-level distractions. Optimize your physical comfort. Persistent physical discomfort creates a constant, subtle pull on your attention. If your chair is uncomfortable, your body will constantly fidget or shift, diverting mental resources. If the room is too cold, you'll be preoccupied with warmth; too hot, and you'll be battling lethargy. Address these fundamental needs first. Invest in an ergonomic chair if possible. Keep a sweater or small fan nearby. Wear comfortable, non-restrictive clothing. The less your body has to complain, the more your mind can focus.

Dedicated Work Zones:

If possible, designate a specific area only for deep work or specific tasks. This cues your brain that when you're in that spot, it's time to focus. Avoid working in bed or on the couch if those spaces are associated with relaxation. Even a specific chair or side of a table can serve this purpose. The principle here is strong environmental association. Your brain learns to associate certain places with certain activities. If you work, relax, eat, and sleep in the same spot, your brain receives mixed signals. By dedicating a "work zone," you train your brain to enter a focused state merely by being in that area. This doesn't mean you need a separate room; it could be a specific desk in a corner, a particular chair, or even just the dining table used *only* for work during certain hours. The consistency of this spatial cue helps trigger your "focus mode."

"Tools In, Distractions Out":

Before starting a task, gather all the tools you'll need (pens, paper, specific documents, water bottle, etc.). Simultaneously, remove all potential distractions (phone in another room, social media tabs closed, irrelevant books put away). This minimizes reasons to break focus. This is a crucial pre-work ritual. The goal is to eliminate any reason to interrupt your flow once you've started. Running to grab a forgotten pen, looking for a file, or realizing you need a drink can all become opportunities for distraction and derailment. Conversely, proactively removing potential distractions *before* you start creates a clear path for your attention. This "preparation phase" helps you transition into focused work smoothly and reduces the cognitive load of decision-making during your work session.

Digital Discipline: Taming the Online World

The digital realm is often the biggest culprit for attention fragmentation for men with ADHD. The internet, with its infinite novelty and instant gratification, is uniquely designed to hijack the ADHD brain's attention. Mastering digital discipline is therefore non-negotiable for sustained focus in the modern world. This requires a proactive and often aggressive approach to managing notifications, browser habits, and smartphone usage.

Notification Annihilation:

This is paramount. Turn off all non-essential notifications on your phone, tablet, and computer. Email, social media, news alerts—they are designed to hijack your attention. Schedule specific times to check them, rather than being at their mercy. Each notification is a micro-interruption that pulls your attention away, even if just for a second. For the ADHD brain, that micro-interruption often leads to a lengthy derailment, as the brain "sticks" to the new stimulus. Be ruthless. Turn off banners, sounds, and badges for anything that isn't absolutely critical. For emails, close your email client unless you are specifically in an "email processing" block. For social media, consider deleting the apps from your phone and only accessing them via a desktop browser during scheduled breaks. The less your devices are constantly vying for your attention, the more mental energy you'll have for your actual work.

Strategic App & Tab Management:

The digital workspace, much like a physical one, can become cluttered and distracting.

- **Browser Extensions:** Use extensions like "StayFocusd" or "Freedom" to block distracting websites during work periods. These tools act as external accountability partners, preventing you from impulsively drifting to time-wasting sites. Set them up to block social media, news sites, or entertainment platforms during your designated work hours. This creates a powerful barrier that bypasses the need for constant willpower.
- **Tab Limiting:** Commit to having only 1-3 tabs open at any given time. Each additional tab is an invitation for distraction. Open tabs are like open loops in your brain, each demanding a piece of your working memory. The more tabs you have, the more visual and mental clutter you create, making it harder to focus on the active task. Cultivate the habit of closing tabs immediately once you're done with them.
- **Dedicated Browsers/Profiles:** Consider having a separate browser (e.g., Firefox for work, Chrome for personal) or different user profiles to keep work and personal browsing separate. This creates a clear boundary between your professional and personal digital life. When you open your

"work browser," your brain receives a strong cue that it's time to focus, as all personal distractions (bookmarks, saved passwords, open tabs) are not immediately available.

Phone Hygiene:

Your smartphone is a powerful tool and a potent distraction. It is arguably the single greatest threat to sustained focus in the modern era.

- **Physical Distance:** Put your phone in another room or a drawer while working. Out of sight, out of mind. This is the most effective strategy. If your phone is within arm's reach or line of sight, the temptation to check it will be constant. By physically separating yourself from it, you remove the immediate cue and significantly reduce the likelihood of impulsive checking.
- **Do Not Disturb Mode:** Use this feature liberally. Customize it to allow calls from emergencies only. This allows you to control who can reach you, preventing unnecessary interruptions while still ensuring you're available for critical contacts.
- **App Organization:** Group distracting apps into folders on your phone's last screen, making them less accessible. Make the process of getting to these apps slightly more cumbersome. The extra taps or swipes can provide just enough friction to engage your executive functions and allow you to reconsider the impulse.

Scheduled Digital Breaks:

Instead of letting digital distractions pull you away randomly, schedule short, intentional breaks (e.g., 5 minutes every hour) to check emails, messages, or social media. This gives your brain permission to look forward to these "release" times. Fighting every urge to check your phone or email is exhausting. By scheduling designated "digital breaks," you legitimize the desire for stimulation but contain it to specific periods. This reduces the constant mental battle and allows you to fully engage with your work during your focused blocks, knowing that a controlled "release" is coming.

Offline First:

Whenever possible, download documents, read articles, or do work that doesn't require an internet connection. Then, disconnect your Wi-Fi. This creates an immediate, strong barrier against online distractions. If your work doesn't absolutely require an internet connection, removing the possibility of online distractions altogether is the ultimate environmental design hack. This forces you to focus only on the materials at hand and eliminates the temptation of endless browsing.

By consciously designing both your physical and digital environments, you are not just reacting to distractions, but proactively building a fortress for your focus. This isn't about perfection, but about creating systems that support your brain's natural tendencies. Take the time to observe your current habits, identify your biggest environmental culprits, and then implement these strategies to clear the runway for sustained, productive attention. This proactive approach transforms your workspace from a source of struggle into a powerful ally, empowering you to achieve deeper concentration and more consistent productivity.

CHAPTER 3:

MINDFULNESS AND PRESENCE FOR ATTENTION

We've explored how to shape your external world for better focus, recognizing that a thoughtfully designed environment can significantly reduce the pull of distractions. Now, we turn inward to cultivate your internal landscape. This is where mindfulness and presence become incredibly powerful tools for the ADHD brain. Often, the greatest distractions aren't external pings and notifications, but the relentless chatter of our own minds—the planning for tomorrow, the regrets of yesterday, the rehashing of past conversations, or the sudden, exciting new idea that pulls you off track with compelling urgency. This internal world, while a source of creativity and spontaneity, can also become a chaotic torrent of thoughts and emotions, making sustained attention a formidable challenge. For men with ADHD, who frequently experience a mind that races ahead, gets stuck in loops, or drifts effortlessly into imaginative realms, mastering this internal terrain is not just beneficial, but transformative.

Mindfulness is simply the practice of paying attention, on purpose, to the present moment, without judgment. It's about observing your thoughts, feelings, and sensations as they arise, rather than getting entangled in them or being carried away by their current. Presence is the natural outcome of mindfulness—a state of being fully engaged with what's happening right now, whether it's a conversation, a task, or a quiet moment of reflection. For men with ADHD, who often experience a mind that races ahead or drifts behind, cultivating mindfulness can feel like learning to gently lasso your runaway thoughts and bring them back to the here and now. It's a process of becoming the observer of your internal experience, rather than being solely subject to its whims. This allows for a crucial pause, a moment of intentionality, before your automatic reactions take over.

This isn't about emptying your mind or achieving some zen-like state of perfect stillness (which is often unrealistic for anyone, let alone someone with ADHD). The ADHD brain is inherently active, a vibrant engine of thought and energy. Trying to force it into absolute stillness is often counterproductive and frustrating. Instead, mindfulness for ADHD is about building your attentional muscle by repeatedly guiding your focus back to the present. Each time your mind wanders and you gently, without self-reproach, bring it back to your chosen anchor or current task, you're doing a "rep" for your attention. This consistent, compassionate redirection strengthens your capacity for sustained focus, making it easier over time to choose where your mental spotlight shines, even amidst internal noise. It's a pragmatic, iterative approach that acknowledges the brain's natural tendencies while gently nudging it towards greater control.

Anchoring Your Attention: Mindfulness Practices

The core of mindfulness for attention is having an "anchor"—something to consistently bring your focus back to when your mind inevitably drifts. For the ADHD brain, which can struggle with internal filtering and sustained mental effort, an accessible and consistent anchor provides a point of return, a home base for your attention amidst the chaos. These practices are not meant to be rigid rituals, but flexible tools to build awareness and control.

The Breath Anchor:

Your breath is always with you and is a constant, subtle sensation. It is perhaps the most fundamental and universally accessible anchor because it is always present, it is neutral, and its rhythm can be both observed and subtly influenced.

- **Simple Breath Focus:** Sit comfortably. Close your eyes or soften your gaze to minimize visual distraction. Bring your attention to the sensation of your breath entering and leaving your body. Notice the rise and fall of your chest or abdomen, the feeling of air at your nostrils, or the gentle expansion and contraction of your diaphragm. When your mind wanders (and it will, relentlessly at first!), gently acknowledge the thought without judgment. Don't criticize yourself for drifting; simply note, "There's a thought about my to-do list," or "My mind has wandered to that conversation." Then, gently, as if guiding a small child, guide your attention back to your breath. Start with 2-5 minutes of this practice daily, perhaps at the beginning of your day or before a challenging task, and gradually increase the duration as your capacity grows. The key is the *gentle return*, not the absence of wandering. Each return is a strengthening of your attentional muscle.

- **Counting Breaths:** As you exhale, count "one." On the next exhale, "two," up to "ten," then start over from "one." If your mind wanders and you lose count, simply start again from "one" without judgment. This adds a gentle, rhythmic structure that can be particularly helpful for a busy or restless mind. The act of counting provides just enough mental engagement to keep the ADHD brain from getting bored, while still directing attention to the breath. It creates a clearer focal point than just "noticing" the breath, offering a tangible metric for your practice.

Sensory Check-Ins (5-4-3-2-1 Method):

When your mind is racing, you feel overwhelmed by internal chatter, or you're stuck in a thought loop, this exercise can quickly ground you in the present by bringing your awareness to external reality.

- **5 things you can see:** Look around and name five distinct things you can see. Focus on details—colors, textures, shapes. (e.g., "the blue of the wall," "the grain of the wooden table," "the dust motes dancing in the sunlight").
- **4 things you can feel:** Notice four things you can feel (e.g., your feet on the floor, the texture of your clothes against your skin, the air temperature, the pressure of your chair). Really lean into the sensation.
- **3 things you can hear:** Listen for three distinct sounds (e.g., distant traffic, your own breathing, the hum of a computer, the chirping of a bird). Don't judge them, just notice their presence.
- **2 things you can smell:** Notice two distinct smells (even if faint, e.g., lingering coffee, fresh air from an open window, the scent of your shirt).
- **1 thing you can taste:** Notice one taste in your mouth (e.g., the lingering taste of your last meal, the freshness from toothpaste, or just your own saliva). This exercise is a rapid, powerful circuit-breaker for an overactive mind. It quickly pulls your attention away from internal distractions, such as worries, regrets, or future planning, and redirects it into your immediate, external reality, providing a quick reset for your attention. It's an excellent tool to use before starting a task, during a moment of overwhelm, or when you notice your mind spiraling.

Mindful Movement:

Integrate mindfulness into physical activity. This is particularly beneficial for the ADHD brain, as movement can help discharge excess energy and provide a tangible anchor for attention.

- **Walking Meditation:** As you walk, shift your attention from your thoughts to the physical sensations of walking. Pay attention to the sensation of your feet touching the ground, the heel-to-toe roll, the swing of your arms, the movement of your legs, and the rhythm of your breath. Notice the sights and sounds around you without labeling or judging them; simply observe. This is an excellent way to combine the benefits of physical activity (which helps regulate dopamine) with attentional training.

- **Mindful Stretching/Yoga:** Focus intensely on the sensations in your body as you stretch or hold a pose. Notice the stretch, the release, the tension, and the relaxation. This can be a great way to combine physical activity with mental anchoring, promoting both body awareness and mental focus. Even simple stretches at your desk can become mindful moments.
- **Mindful Eating/Drinking:** Instead of mindlessly consuming food or drink, choose one meal or beverage a day to practice mindful eating. Before you even take a bite or sip, notice the colors, textures, smells. As you chew, pay attention to the taste, the temperature, how the food feels in your mouth, and the act of swallowing. Chew slowly, savoring each bite. This engages multiple senses and trains your attention by slowing down a common, often rushed activity, fostering a deeper connection to the present moment.

Integrating Presence into Daily Life: Beyond Formal Practice

Mindfulness isn't just for meditation cushions or structured exercises; it's a way of approaching everyday moments, transforming routine activities into opportunities for attentional training and greater presence. The goal is to weave moments of conscious awareness throughout your day, making presence a habit rather than an occasional event.

The "One-Minute Mindfulness Break":

Set an alarm for once or twice an hour, or at natural transition points in your day (e.g., when a meeting ends, before starting a new task). When it goes off, pause whatever you're doing. Take three deep breaths, focusing on the sensation of each breath. Look around you and notice one thing you haven't seen before, or one detail you often overlook. Then return to your task.

This acts as a micro-reset for your attention, preventing mental fatigue, reducing accumulation of internal distractions, and bringing you back to the present moment before you get completely derailed. It's a powerful way to integrate consistent "attentional reps" without needing long, dedicated meditation sessions.

Active Listening:

In conversations, make a conscious effort to truly listen to the other person, rather than planning your response, letting your mind drift, or formulating counter-arguments. When you notice your mind wandering, gently bring it back to their words. Try to silently paraphrase what they've said in your head to ensure comprehension and active engagement.

For men with ADHD, rapid-fire thinking often means your brain is already three steps ahead, anticipating the conversation's direction or formulating your next brilliant point. This can lead to interrupting, missing crucial details, or others feeling unheard. Practicing engaged listening not only improves your relationships but also trains your sustained attention in a real-world, dynamic context. Ask open-ended questions to encourage the other person to elaborate, which further anchors your attention.

Single-Task Awareness:

As you work on a task, bring your full, conscious attention to it. When you notice your mind drifting (and it *will*), acknowledge the distraction without judgment ("There's a thought about what to eat for lunch"). Then, gently but firmly redirect your attention back to the task. This is the "attentional rep" in action – each time you bring your attention back, you strengthen the neural pathways for focus. Avoid multitasking, as it fragments attention and reduces efficiency for the ADHD brain. Commit to one task at a time, and every time your mind pulls away, practice the gentle return. Over time, the periods of sustained single-task focus will naturally lengthen.

The "Curiosity Mindset":

Approach tasks, even mundane or boring ones, with a sense of genuine curiosity. What can you learn from this? What details can you observe? What is the underlying mechanism? Engaging your natural curiosity can make mundane tasks more palatable and easier to focus on by providing an internal source of stimulation. For example, if you're doing paperwork, instead of just seeing "forms," observe the design of the form, the font, the sequence of information. If you're washing dishes, notice the temperature of the water, the feel of the soap, the shine of the clean plate. This approach injects novelty and engagement into tasks that might otherwise feel under-stimulating, leveraging your brain's natural inclination towards new information.

Acknowledge and Let Go:

When distracting thoughts or emotions arise, instead of fighting them or getting lost in them, simply acknowledge their presence ("There's a thought about X," "I'm feeling impatient," "There's an urge to check my phone"). Then, consciously choose to let them go and return your attention to your anchor or your task. Trying to suppress thoughts often makes them stronger, like trying not to think about a pink elephant. Instead, practice non-judgmental observation: observe the thought or emotion as if it's a cloud passing by in the sky. You notice it, but you don't jump on it and ride it away. By acknowledging without engagement, you weaken its power to hijack your attention and reinforce your capacity to choose where your focus lies. This is a subtle but profoundly effective self-regulation skill.

Cultivating mindfulness and presence is a lifelong practice, not a quick fix or a destination. For men with ADHD, it offers a powerful pathway to greater control over your attention, reduced reactivity, and a richer, more engaged experience of the present moment. By regularly training your internal spotlight, you'll find it easier to direct your focus where you intend, even in a world clamoring for your attention and a mind prone to wandering. This internal mastery is a vital complement to designing your external environment for sustained focus, creating a holistic approach that empowers you to truly take command of your attention and, by extension, your life. The journey is ongoing, but the rewards of greater presence and control are immeasurable.

CHAPTER 4:

SINGLE-TASKING AND DEEP WORK STRATEGIES

We've explored how to shape your external world for better focus by designing an environment conducive to concentration, and we've begun to cultivate your internal landscape through mindfulness and presence, anchoring your attention to the present moment. Now, it's time to put those principles into practice with some of the most potent strategies for sustained focus: single-tasking and deep work. In a world that constantly pushes for multitasking, these approaches are revolutionary, especially for the ADHD brain. The pervasive myth that juggling multiple tasks simultaneously enhances productivity is deeply ingrained in modern work culture. However, for an ADHD brain, constantly switching between tasks is not just inefficient; it's actively detrimental. Each switch depletes valuable mental energy, fragments attention, and leads to more errors, superficial work, and less actual completed output. This "context switching cost" is astronomically higher for an ADHD brain, as the effort required to disengage from one task and re-engage with another is immense, often involving a significant "reboot" of mental resources and a hunt for the necessary dopamine to kickstart the new activity.

Single-tasking is simply the practice of focusing on one task at a time, giving it your undivided attention until it's complete or a designated time period ends. It's a deliberate act of choosing singularity over fragmentation. Deep work, a term coined by author Cal Newport in his seminal book, takes this a step further: it's the ability to focus without distraction on a cognitively demanding task. It's the kind of work that creates new value, improves your skills, and is difficult to replicate, requiring sustained intellectual effort at the highest level. For the ADHD brain, achieving this state of deep work is not always easy, given its natural inclination towards novelty and immediate stimulation, but it is profoundly rewarding. The moments of true deep work are where innovation happens, where complex problems are solved, and where significant personal and professional growth occurs. It's the antithesis of the shallow, fragmented work that often characterizes modern productivity.

The challenge lies in your brain's natural inclination for novelty and stimulation. A single, demanding task, especially if it involves sustained effort and lacks immediate gratification, can quickly feel boring or difficult, prompting your mind to seek out more immediate dopamine hits from distractions. The prefrontal cortex, responsible for executive functions like sustained attention, relies on dopamine for optimal functioning. When a task isn't providing enough novel stimulation, the brain's dopamine levels may dip, leading to a search for external stimulation (distractions) to get that quick hit. This makes single-tasking and deep work feel like pushing against a strong current. However, by deliberately engaging in single-tasking and structuring your environment and time for deep work, you can train your brain to embrace sustained effort and achieve higher levels of productivity and satisfaction. You are not fighting your brain but *teaching* it to find reward in sustained, focused effort through structured practice and strategic reinforcement.

The Power of One: Embracing Single-Tasking

The core principle here is simplicity and dedication. It's about stripping away unnecessary complexity and committing fully to the task at hand. This approach counteracts the ADHD brain's tendency to scatter attention and provides a clear, unwavering target for your mental energy.

- **Identify Your One Task:** Before you begin a work session, clearly decide on the single task you will focus on. Write it down. Make it specific and tangible. For example, instead of "work on report," choose "write introduction for report" or "outline Chapter 2 of the proposal." The specificity reduces ambiguity and decision fatigue, which are significant energy drains for the ADHD brain. Having only one designated task on your mental radar provides immense relief, as your brain doesn't have to constantly juggle competing priorities or wonder what to do next. This clear focus point makes initiation easier and reduces the likelihood of immediate distraction.

- **Eliminate All Other Options:** This is where environmental design and digital discipline from Chapter 2 come into play with full force. Close all irrelevant tabs, put your phone on silent and out of reach (ideally in another room or a drawer), close your email client and messaging apps, and clear your physical workspace of anything not pertaining to that one task. Make it physically and digitally difficult to switch. Use browser extensions that block distracting websites during your focus sessions. Turn your chair to face a blank wall if necessary. The fewer opportunities your brain has to wander to an easier, more stimulating alternative, the more likely it is to engage with the designated task. This external barrier reduces the reliance on willpower, which is a finite resource.

- **Use a Timer (The Pomodoro Technique Refined):** This is perhaps the most effective single-tasking tool for ADHD because it works *with* the brain's need for novelty and breaks, rather than fighting against it.

- Set a timer for 25 minutes (your "Pomodoro"). This short, manageable burst of time feels less daunting than an open-ended work session, making initiation easier.
- Commit to working *only* on your chosen task for that entire duration. This is the core of single-tasking. If a distracting thought arises (and it will!), quickly jot it down on a "Distraction List" (a simple piece of paper next to you) and immediately return to your task. Do *not* act on the distraction; simply externalize it for later. This honors the thought without allowing it to derail your current focus.
- When the timer rings, take a mandatory 5-minute break. Get up, stretch, grab water, look out a window, or do a quick mindful body scan. Critically, do *not* check email, social media, or get involved in another task during this short break. This break is designed for mental reset, not for new stimulation.
- After four Pomodoros, take a longer break (20-30 minutes). Use this time for more substantial recovery, checking messages, or engaging in a short, preferred activity. The power of this technique for ADHD lies in its structured breaks, which provide regular dopamine hits, and its defined work periods, which manage the feeling of overwhelm. It trains your brain to focus intensely for short, manageable bursts, gradually extending your capacity for sustained attention.

- **Batch Similar Tasks:** While the goal is single-tasking *within* a work session, you can still improve efficiency by batching similar tasks together across your day or week. For example, dedicate a specific block of time solely to answering emails, another block for making phone calls, and yet another for administrative paperwork. This minimizes the "context switching" cost: the mental energy wasted when your brain has to constantly reorient itself to different types of tasks and different cognitive demands. By grouping similar activities, you allow your brain to stay in a particular "mode," reducing the

friction and cognitive load associated with frequent transitions.
- **Focus on "Inputs" Not Just "Outputs":** For highly challenging or overwhelming tasks, sometimes the "output" (e.g., finishing the whole report, completing a complex coding project) feels too daunting, leading to procrastination or task paralysis. Instead, shift your focus to the "input" you need to provide: "I will work on this report for 45 minutes," or "I will read 2 chapters of this book," or "I will write 200 words." This shifts your brain's focus from a potentially overwhelming, distant goal to a manageable, immediate action. This approach reduces the pressure for perfectionism, makes initiation easier, and allows your brain to find satisfaction in the act of *doing* rather than solely in the completed product. The momentum generated by consistent input often naturally leads to the desired output.

Creating Your Deep Work Sanctuary: Strategic Implementation

Deep work requires more than just willpower; it requires strategic planning and protection. It's about proactively carving out and defending periods of uninterrupted, focused effort, creating a "sanctuary" where your most demanding cognitive work can flourish.

- **Schedule Deep Work Blocks:** Don't wait for inspiration or a sudden burst of motivation; schedule your deep work time just like you would a critical meeting. Identify your peak focus times (often mornings for many with ADHD, before the day's distractions fully set in) and block out 1-2 hour segments for your most demanding, cognitively intensive tasks. Treat these blocks as sacred, non-negotiable appointments in your calendar. Use a different color in your digital calendar or physically block out the time. This intentional scheduling reduces decision fatigue and signals to your brain that this period is dedicated to focused effort.
- **Communicate Your Intent:** If you work in an open office, share a workspace, or live with others, communicate your deep work periods clearly. Put up a "Do Not Disturb" sign, use headphones (a universal signal for focus), or let family

members know you need uninterrupted time for specific blocks. Be explicit about your need for quiet and lack of interruption. Setting clear boundaries with colleagues, family, and friends protects your focus blocks from external encroachment. Consider using a tool like Slack's "Do Not Disturb" feature or setting an auto-responder on your email to manage expectations.

- **The "Pre-Flight Checklist":** Before starting a deep work session, develop a brief, consistent ritual or "pre-flight checklist." This ritual cues your brain that it's time to engage in sustained focus and helps you smoothly transition into deep work. This could include:
    - Reviewing your single, specific task for the session.
    - Gathering all necessary materials (documents, specific software, water, a light snack).
    - Getting a fresh drink of water or coffee.
    - Closing all unnecessary programs, tabs, and silencing *all* notifications.
    - Doing a quick 60-second mindfulness check-in (as discussed in Chapter 3) to ground yourself. This consistent ritual acts as a psychological trigger, preparing your mind and body for intense concentration.
- **Limit "Shallow Work" Time:** Shallow work, such as checking email, administrative tasks, casual meetings, or responding to messages, is necessary but often less demanding and more prone to distraction. For the ADHD brain, shallow work can be a dopamine trap, providing frequent, small hits of gratification that deter you from tackling more challenging, less immediately rewarding deep work. Consciously limit the time you spend on these activities, perhaps grouping them into specific "shallow work blocks" outside of your prime deep work hours. Process email only 2-3 times a day, for example, rather than having it open constantly. This protects your most valuable mental energy for the tasks that truly move the needle.

- **Build in Recovery Time:** Deep work is mentally taxing. Just as you wouldn't expect to run a marathon every day, don't expect to do intense deep work for eight hours straight. Schedule regular, meaningful breaks between sessions and allow for ample recovery time between deep work blocks, and certainly at the end of the day. This prevents cognitive burnout, replenishes mental energy, and maintains your ability to engage in focused work over the long term. Recovery could involve physical movement, spending time in nature, engaging in a non-stimulating hobby, or simply resting. For the ADHD brain, understanding the need for rest and actively building it into your schedule is crucial for sustainable productivity.

- **Review and Reflect:** After a deep work session (or at the end of the day), briefly reflect on how it went. What helped you stay focused? What were the biggest distractions or challenges? What can you adjust for the next session? Did you manage your Pomodoro breaks effectively? Did you honor your single-task commitment? This iterative learning is key to refining your deep work habits. By consistently analyzing your performance, you gain valuable insights into your personal focus triggers and distractions, allowing you to continuously optimize your environment and strategies. This self-awareness accelerates your mastery of deep work.

Embracing single-tasking and deep work is a powerful counter-cultural act in our hyper-connected world, and it's especially transformative for men with ADHD. By deliberately creating mental and environmental space for sustained focus on one thing at a time, you'll not only complete more meaningful work but also experience a profound sense of accomplishment and clarity, moving beyond the chaos of constant distraction. This intentional approach allows you to harness your considerable potential, achieving a level of productivity and satisfaction that might have previously seemed out of reach.

CHAPTER 5:

SUSTAINING FOCUS AND PREVENTING BURNOUT

You've learned to understand the ADHD focus challenge, designed your environment for optimal concentration, cultivated mindfulness to anchor your internal attention, and implemented powerful single-tasking and deep work strategies. These are foundational tools for getting into a state of sustained focus. But what happens after that intense period of concentration? How do you maintain that newfound ability without hitting a wall of exhaustion, or worse, burning out completely? This final chapter in Book 2 addresses the crucial, often overlooked, aspect of the focus equation: sustaining your attention over the long haul and building resilience against mental fatigue. It's not enough to be able to access deep focus; the true mastery lies in managing your energy and protecting your well-being so that these periods of intense concentration are sustainable, consistent, and ultimately contribute to a flourishing life, rather than leading to a crash.

For men with ADHD, the pursuit of focus can sometimes feel like a high-stakes sprint. The effort required to overcome internal and external distractions, initiate challenging tasks, and maintain cognitive grip can be immense, leading to disproportionate mental exhaustion, irritability, and even a feeling of being "fried." This is particularly true if you rely heavily on stimulating activities (like hyper-focusing, external novelty, or last-minute adrenaline rushes) to get things done, rather than building sustainable attentional habits rooted in consistent energy management. The ADHD brain often operates on a feast-or-famine cycle regarding stimulation and dopamine. Periods of intense, unmanaged focus, especially hyperfocus, can neglect fundamental needs like eating, sleeping, or taking breaks, leading to a significant energy debt. Without proper recovery and self-care, this cycle can quickly lead to reduced productivity, increased stress and anxiety, heightened symptom severity (e.g., more distractibility, greater impulsivity), and an inevitable return to old patterns of scattered attention and avoidance. The consequence is not just lost productivity, but a significant toll on mental and physical health.

Sustaining focus isn't just about the moments you're "on" and working intensely; it's about optimizing your entire daily rhythm to support your attention. It's about recognizing the subtle signs of fatigue, proactively managing your energy levels throughout the day, and building a lifestyle that allows your brain to perform at its best without succumbing to the relentless demands of modern life. This holistic approach acknowledges that focus is deeply intertwined with overall well-being, and that neglecting one will inevitably compromise the other. It's about proactive maintenance, not just reactive repair.

Fueling Your Focus: Energy Management Strategies

Think of your focus as a finite resource, much like a battery. You need to consistently charge it, use it wisely, and prevent it from running completely flat. Ignoring these fundamental inputs is akin to trying to drive a car with an empty fuel tank or a failing engine—no amount of driving skill will make it perform.

Strategic Breaks (Beyond Pomodoro):

While Pomodoro breaks (as discussed in Chapter 4) are excellent for short, focused bursts, you need longer, more restorative breaks tailored to the unique needs of the ADHD brain. These breaks are not a luxury but a necessity for cognitive replenishment.

- **Micro-Breaks:** Every 15-20 minutes, take a 30-second to 1-minute "brain break." Look away from your screen, stretch, take a few deep breaths, or simply close your eyes. This prevents cognitive overload and the build-up of mental fatigue by allowing for brief moments of cognitive disengagement. For the ADHD brain, which processes so much stimuli, these micro-pauses prevent overstimulation and allow your prefrontal cortex a brief moment of rest.

- **Movement Breaks:** Stand up, walk around, do some push-ups or squats every hour. Physical movement boosts circulation, increases blood flow to the brain, and helps regulate neurotransmitters like dopamine and norepinephrine, effectively re-energizing your brain and combating the mental stagnation of prolonged sitting. Movement can also help discharge restless energy that often accompanies ADHD, making it easier to return to a focused state.

- **Nature Breaks:** If possible, step outside for 5-10 minutes. Even looking at a tree, feeling the sun on your face, or hearing the sounds of birds can be incredibly restorative for your attention. "Green space" exposure has been shown to reduce mental fatigue and improve cognitive function, offering a powerful antidote to screen-induced brain drain.

Optimize Sleep:

This is foundational, not optional. Chronic sleep deprivation is a major enemy of focus, emotional regulation, and impulse control for everyone, but especially for those with ADHD, whose brains are already working harder to self-regulate. Prioritize consistent, quality sleep (7-9 hours for most adults). Create a relaxing bedtime routine (e.g., dimming lights, reading a physical book, taking a warm bath) that signals to your body it's time to wind down. Ensure your bedroom is dark, quiet, and cool, and avoid screens (phones, tablets, computers, TV) for at least 60-90 minutes before bed, as their blue light interferes with melatonin production. Sleep is when your brain cleanses itself and consolidates learning; sacrificing it directly impairs your next day's cognitive function.

Nutrition and Hydration:

Your brain needs consistent, high-quality fuel to function optimally. Dehydration and erratic blood sugar levels can wreak havoc on your attention and mood, mimicking or exacerbating ADHD symptoms. Drink plenty of water throughout the day, aiming for consistent hydration rather than large infrequent intakes. Opt for balanced meals with lean protein (for sustained amino acid supply), healthy fats (crucial for brain cell membranes), and complex carbohydrates (for steady glucose release) to maintain stable energy levels and prevent energy crashes. Avoid excessive simple sugars and highly processed foods, which lead to rapid blood sugar spikes and subsequent crashes, leaving you feeling sluggish and unfocused.

Mindful Consumption of Stimulants:

Caffeine, nicotine, and even some ADHD medications are stimulants. While they can be powerful tools for focus, their effects can be a double-edged sword for ADHD. Pay close attention to how caffeine specifically affects your focus, anxiety levels, and sleep. Some individuals with ADHD find it helpful in moderate doses, while others experience increased anxiety or a significant "crash" later in the day that severely impairs focus. Consider when and how much you consume, avoiding caffeine late in the day. Be aware of the "post-caffeine crash," which can lead to increased irritability and difficulty concentrating. Experiment with different types and amounts, and observe your personal response to find your optimal balance.

Regular Physical Activity:

Exercise is a natural mood and focus enhancer, often likened to "medication for ADHD" due to its profound neurochemical benefits. It increases dopamine and norepinephrine, helps regulate energy levels, reduces restlessness, and improves sleep quality. Find an activity you genuinely enjoy and make it a consistent part of your routine. This could be lifting weights, running, cycling, team sports, hiking, or even brisk walking. Even 20-30 minutes of moderate activity most days can make a significant difference in your ability to initiate tasks, sustain attention, and manage emotional regulation throughout the day. Exercise helps to both release pent-up energy and provide a calming, regulating effect on the brain.

Building Resilience: Protecting Against Burnout

Burnout is not just about being tired; it's a state of chronic physical, emotional, and mental exhaustion caused by prolonged or excessive stress. For men with ADHD, the constant effort to manage symptoms, fight distractions, regulate emotions, and navigate a demanding world can make you particularly susceptible to this debilitating state. Building resilience is about creating buffers and practices that protect your vital energy reserves.

Recognize Your Burnout Signals:

Learn your personal warning signs. Early detection is key to intervention. Are you more irritable than usual, snapping at loved ones? Having significantly more trouble initiating tasks, even simple ones? Feeling cynical or detached from your work or hobbies? Experiencing increased forgetfulness or "brain fog"? Are you withdrawing socially? Are you experiencing physical symptoms like persistent headaches, stomach issues, frequent colds, or muscle tension? Catching these subtle cues early allows you to intervene before full burnout sets in, enabling you to step back and recharge proactively. Keep a simple journal to track your mood and energy levels if you find it hard to identify patterns.

Schedule True Downtime:

This isn't just "not working" or collapsing on the couch to scroll aimlessly. True downtime is intentionally unplugging and engaging in activities that genuinely recharge you, providing restorative rest for your mind and body. This might include engaging in hobbies (without turning them into another "task"), spending time in nature, pursuing creative outlets, connecting meaningfully with loved ones without distraction, or simply doing nothing active. Treat downtime as important as work time; schedule it in your calendar and defend it vigorously. For the ADHD brain, which is prone to overstimulation, true downtime means disengaging from screens and mentally demanding activities to allow for quiet processing and restoration.

Practice Realistic Self-Expectations:

Avoid the trap of perfectionism or constantly comparing yourself to neurotypical productivity standards. Acknowledge and accept your brain's unique wiring and its inherent challenges. It's okay to have "off" days where focus is elusive, or when you don't achieve everything on your to-do list. Be kind to yourself when things don't go as planned; harsh self-criticism only depletes the emotional and cognitive resources needed for regulation and resilience. Focus on consistent, sustainable effort and progress, rather than unrealistic bursts of productivity or unattainable ideals. Celebrate small wins and acknowledge the effort involved in managing ADHD symptoms. Self-compassion is a powerful antidote to the shame and frustration that can fuel burnout.

Delegate and Say No:

Learn to identify tasks that can be delegated or opportunities that you need to politely decline. Men with ADHD can sometimes overcommit due to enthusiasm, difficulty estimating time requirements, or a desire to please. Overcommitment is a fast track to overwhelm and burnout, especially when you have ADHD, as it stretches your limited executive function resources too thin. Protect your energy and time for your true priorities. Practice saying "No" to new commitments by having polite scripts ready (e.g., "I appreciate you thinking of me, but I'm fully committed right now," or "I need to check my schedule before I can commit, I'll get back to you"). This empowers you to manage your boundaries effectively.

Cultivate a Support System:

You don't have to navigate this alone. Connect with friends, family, a partner, or support groups who understand ADHD. Having people you can talk to openly, share challenges with, and receive encouragement and practical advice from can be a powerful buffer against stress, isolation, and burnout. Consider joining an online or in-person ADHD support group, or seek out a coach or therapist specializing in ADHD. Sharing your experiences and learning from others can validate your struggles and provide fresh perspectives and strategies, reinforcing that you are not alone in your journey.

Review and Reflect on Your Focus Habits:

At the end of each day or week, briefly reflect on how your focus strategies worked. What enabled you to sustain focus? What led to fatigue or distraction? Were your breaks restorative? Did you honor your boundaries? This continuous learning process allows you to refine your approach, making your focus efforts more efficient and less draining over time. This meta-awareness, a core component of executive function, allows you to become an active, informed manager of your own attention and energy. Use a simple journal or a mental check-in to periodically assess and adapt your strategies.

Sustaining focus isn't a relentless grind; it's a mindful dance between intense effort and intelligent recovery. By implementing these strategies for energy management and burnout prevention, you'll not only extend your capacity for attention and productivity but also foster a deeper sense of well-being, resilience, and personal control. This integrated approach ensures that your sharpened focus becomes a consistent, reliable asset, helping you thrive in a world that constantly vies for your attention, rather than merely survive it. It's about building a life where focus is a tool for flourishing, not a pathway to exhaustion.

CONCLUSION:
YOUR FOCUSED EDGE

You've now completed Book 2, "Mastering Focus: Sustained Attention in a Distracting World," and in doing so, you've equipped yourself with a profound understanding of how to harness your attention in a world designed for distraction. We've journeyed from dissecting the unique ways the ADHD brain approaches focus to implementing tangible strategies that empower you to direct and sustain your mental spotlight.

You've learned to:

- **Deconstruct the ADHD focus challenge**, recognizing it not as a personal failing, but as a neurological difference that can be strategically managed.
- **Design your environment** for optimal concentration, transforming both your physical and digital spaces into powerful allies for deep work.
- **Cultivate mindfulness and presence**, anchoring your attention to the present moment and gently guiding your mind back when it wanders.
- **Master single-tasking and deep work**, embracing the power of focused effort on one thing at a time, rather than falling prey to the myth of multitasking.
- **Sustain your focus and prevent burnout**, understanding that consistent attention is built on smart energy management, strategic breaks, and genuine self-care.

This focused edge isn't about eradicating your ADHD; it's about learning to work *with* your brain's unique rhythms. It's about empowering you to choose where your attention goes, rather than being pulled by every fleeting impulse or external demand. You're building resilience, enhancing your capacity for deep work, and ultimately, gaining a significant advantage in achieving your goals and living a more intentional life.

The strategies covered in this book are not one-time fixes; they are practices to be integrated into your daily routine. Experiment with them, adapt them to your personal style, and observe their impact. There will be days of effortless flow and days of struggle, but with each mindful effort, you're strengthening your attentional muscles and creating a more reliable, consistent ability to focus.

As you move forward, carry these principles with you. Your ability to direct your attention is one of your most valuable assets. Continue to protect it, nourish it, and deploy it with purpose. You now have the blueprint to navigate a distracting world with a sharper, more sustained focus, giving you a distinct advantage in all your endeavors.

Let's pause for a moment and reflect on what you've just read. What resonates with you? What are the strategies you feel you can apply to work and life now versus those that seem more challenging or daunting?

BOOK THREE:

UNLEASHING PRODUCTIVITY:
TURNING INTENTIONS INTO ACCOMPLISHMENTS

CHAPTER 1:

REDEFINING PRODUCTIVITY FOR ADHD MEN

You've honed your executive functions, transforming your brain's command center from a chaotic control room into a more organized and effective hub. You've sharpened your focus, gaining greater influence over your attention and learning to direct your mental spotlight with intentionality. Now, it's time to channel that cultivated power into tangible results. This book, "Unleashing Productivity," isn't about simply doing more; it's about redefining productivity for the ADHD brain: moving beyond the conventional, often frustrating, metrics to a personalized system that truly works for you, aligning your unique cognitive landscape with meaningful output. It's about working smarter, with less friction, and achieving a sustainable sense of accomplishment.

For many men, particularly in a culture that glorifies endless grind and quantifiable output, productivity is often measured by a relentless pursuit of a never-ending to-do list, hours meticulously clocked, or the sheer volume of tasks completed. Success is frequently equated with being perpetually busy, with visible output being the ultimate arbiter of worth. For someone with ADHD, this traditional definition can be a source of immense frustration, self-criticism, and even profound shame. You might recognize yourself in the pattern of having bursts of incredible output: Moments of hyperfocus where you achieve in hours what might take others days, only to be followed by periods of overwhelm, crippling procrastination, or the maddening inability to translate brilliant ideas and urgent intentions into concrete, consistent actions. It's a common experience to feel like you're working harder, expending immense mental effort just to initiate or stay on track, but not necessarily smarter, leaving a trail of unfinished projects, missed opportunities, and unmet goals. This often leads to a crushing sense of inadequacy, a feeling that despite your intelligence and effort, you are perpetually "behind" or "not enough."

The challenge isn't a lack of desire, intelligence, or even capability. It stems directly from the inherent difficulties with executive functions we discussed in Book 1 (like planning, initiation, working memory, and emotional regulation) and the unique focus patterns explored in Book 2. Your brain might thrive on novelty, urgency, and high-intensity stimulation, making sustained, methodical, and often repetitive progress a significant hurdle. The very tasks that require consistent, unglamorous effort often feel under-stimulating for the ADHD brain, prompting it to seek out more immediate dopamine hits from distractions or more exciting, albeit less critical, new endeavors. The conventional wisdom often prescribed by productivity gurus, "just push through" or "use more willpower," frequently backfires for someone with ADHD, leading not to breakthrough, but to rapid mental exhaustion, increased anxiety, and ultimately, burnout. This is because it asks the ADHD brain to function against its natural wiring, without providing the necessary support structures or understanding of its unique needs.

So, how do we redefine productivity in a way that truly serves the ADHD brain? It's about shifting from a sole emphasis on raw quantity to a focus on quality, consistency, and, most critically, alignment with your unique strengths and energetic fluctuations. It's a more compassionate, effective, and sustainable approach that respects your neurobiology. This redefinition involves several key paradigm shifts:

- **Understanding your personal energy cycles and attention patterns, including the common experience of time perception challenges (often referred to as 'time blindness'):** This means recognizing that your brain's internal clock might operate differently from a neurotypical one, often struggling to accurately perceive the passage of time, estimate how long tasks will take, or grasp the immediacy of future deadlines. This can lead to chronic lateness, underestimation of task duration, and a feeling that deadlines suddenly appear out of nowhere. Simultaneously, your attentional capacity isn't a constant. You likely have periods of peak alertness and focus (your "prime time") and periods of lower energy and increased distractibility. Redefining productivity means learning to identify these unique fluctuations—when your brain is naturally more engaged, when it needs a break, and when it's better suited for administrative or less demanding tasks, and then working *with* these unique fluctuations, not against them. This involves employing external aids and strategies (like visual timers, breaking tasks into smaller chunks, and scheduling accordingly) to compensate for internal time perception challenges and leverage your natural energy ebbs and flows.
- **Celebrating momentum over perfection:** For many with ADHD, the pursuit of perfection can be a significant barrier to initiation and completion. The "all-or-nothing" thinking pattern can lead to paralysis: if it can't be done perfectly, it might not be started at all, or an almost-finished project remains incomplete because of the perceived need for a flawless final touch. Redefining productivity means recognizing that progress, however small, however imperfect, is infinitely more valuable than paralysis caused by aiming for flawless execution. The goal is to build consistent momentum. Acknowledge that "done is better than perfect," especially in initial stages. The act of simply starting, or completing a rough

draft, builds crucial momentum and provides a sense of accomplishment that fuels further action. This shifts the focus from an intimidating, distant ideal to a series of manageable, achievable steps.

- **Creating sustainable systems:** For the ADHD brain, which often struggles with working memory, organization, and consistent follow-through, relying solely on willpower is a recipe for exhaustion and frustration. Redefining productivity means developing habits, routines, and external structures, such as consistent schedules, organizational frameworks, and automated reminders, that reduce decision fatigue and friction. These systems act as external scaffolding, compensating for internal challenges and making it easier to start tasks, follow through, and manage information without constant conscious effort. When a process is systematized, your brain doesn't have to expend energy reinventing the wheel each time, freeing up mental energy for the actual work that truly matters. This creates a predictable and reliable environment that supports consistent output.

- **Prioritizing impact over activity:** A common ADHD productivity trap is getting caught in "busywork": tasks that feel productive because they keep you occupied, but don't genuinely move you towards your most important goals. This can stem from a desire for immediate gratification from checking off easy tasks, or from getting lost in the details rather than focusing on the bigger picture. Redefining productivity means consciously shifting your focus to tasks that genuinely create the most impact, that align with your highest priorities, and that move you significantly closer to your long-term aspirations. It's about becoming a strategic filter, learning to differentiate between high-leverage activities and those that merely keep you spinning your wheels. This requires clear goal setting and regular evaluation of where your efforts are truly making a difference.

- **Acknowledging and leveraging your ADHD strengths:** This is perhaps the most empowering aspect of redefining productivity. Instead of viewing ADHD solely as a deficit, recognize that your neurodiversity comes with inherent strengths that can be harnessed for extraordinary output when managed strategically. Your rapid thinking, ability to make novel connections, natural curiosity, boundless creativity, entrepreneurial spirit, and capacity to hyperfocus when engaged are not weaknesses; they are powerful assets. Redefining productivity involves understanding how to integrate these strengths into your workflow. For instance, leveraging hyperfocus for deep dives into engaging projects, using rapid idea generation for brainstorming sessions, or channeling your novelty-seeking into exploring new, innovative solutions. This shifts the narrative from "what's wrong with me?" to "how can I maximize my unique potential?"

This isn't about becoming a productivity robot or forcing yourself into a rigid, soul-crushing routine that extinguishes your spontaneity and creativity. Instead, it's about building a compassionate, effective framework that helps you turn intentions into accomplishments consistently, with less stress and more satisfaction. It's about recognizing that your optimal productivity system will be uniquely yours, a reflection of your individual brain and preferences. We will explore how to break down overwhelming tasks into manageable steps, conquer the inertia of procrastination, optimize your workflow to minimize friction, and build robust systems that support your unique way of working, rather than trying to fit you into a conventional mold.

Get ready to shed the guilt of "not enough" and the frustration of "should be doing more." Embrace a powerful, personalized approach to productivity that truly works for your ADHD brain. By the end of this book, you'll have a clear roadmap to unleash your potential, transform your aspirations into tangible achievements, and cultivate a sustainable sense of accomplishment that honors your unique neurodiversity. You will learn to move beyond merely coping, to truly thriving in your work and life.

CHAPTER 2:

TASK BREAKDOWN AND ACTIONABLE STEPS

You've redefined productivity, understanding that it's about smart, consistent action tailored to your ADHD brain, rather than a relentless pursuit of endless tasks. You've acknowledged your unique strengths and the challenges posed by executive function differences and fluctuating focus. Now, let's get practical. One of the biggest and most persistent roadblocks to turning intentions into tangible accomplishments is the sheer overwhelming nature of a large, complex task. When your brain sees something like "Write Book," "Launch New

Product," or "Complete Annual Report" on a to-do list, it often translates that formidable entry into an "Impossible Mountain to Climb." This perception triggers an immediate shutdown response, leading to intense feelings of overwhelm, paralyzing anxiety, or the familiar spiral of procrastination. The solution? Task breakdown – a systematic and powerful process of transforming that intimidating mountain into a series of manageable, actionable, and psychologically approachable steps.

For men with ADHD, the ability to break down tasks is not just a useful skill; it's an essential survival strategy for navigating work and life effectively. Your working memory, which is often a significant challenge in ADHD, can struggle with holding too many complex parts of a project simultaneously. When a task is too big and vague, your brain is forced to juggle an immense amount of information and potential steps, leading to mental clutter and a sense of being lost before you even begin. Furthermore, your task initiation often falters when faced with an abstract, enormous goal that lacks clear, immediate entry points. The "start button" for the ADHD brain requires a spark of clarity and achievable steps. By systematically dissecting a large task into its constituent components, you create clear, distinct entry points that reduce cognitive load, increase motivation by providing frequent small wins, and offer a tangible, visual sense of progress that fuels continued effort. This process bypasses the overwhelm and provides the necessary structure that your brain craves to move forward.

Think of it like dismantling a complex machine. You wouldn't try to move the whole thing at once, or even figure out how to operate it without understanding its parts. Instead, you'd logically identify the smaller components, understand how they fit together, and then work on one piece at a time. This process not only makes the task less daunting but also clarifies the exact, concrete actions needed to move forward. Each step becomes a small, self-contained mission, rather than an overwhelming segment of an endless journey. This methodical approach is precisely what helps the ADHD brain gain traction and maintain momentum.

The Art of Dissection: How to Break Down Any Task

The goal here is to get from a vague idea or an amorphous project to a series of concrete, "doable" actions that are easy to initiate and complete. This process externalizes the cognitive burden, leveraging your visual and kinesthetic senses to support your planning.

- **The "Mind Map" or "Brain Dump" Start:** Begin by writing down the main task or project at the center of a large space. Then, brainstorm *everything* and anything associated with it, letting your thoughts flow freely without censorship. Don't worry about order, logic, or completeness at this stage. Just get all the sub-ideas, related concepts, questions that arise, known steps, potential obstacles, resources needed, and even anxieties out of your head and onto a visual medium. Use a large whiteboard, a big piece of paper, sticky notes, or a digital mind-mapping tool (like MindMeister, XMind, or even a simple bullet-point list in a note app). This "brain dump" serves a crucial purpose: it externalizes the cognitive burden from your working memory, freeing up mental space and allowing you to see the entire landscape of the project, no matter how chaotic it initially appears. It's the first step in taming the mental storm.

- **Identify the Major Phases/Categories:** Look at your brainstormed, often messy, list. Can you group related items into logical phases or overarching categories? For example, for "Plan a Trip to Europe," categories might naturally emerge: "Research Destinations," "Book Flights," "Book Accommodation," "Create Itinerary," "Pack," "Budgeting," "Visa & Documentation." For "Write a Business Proposal," categories could be: "Research Market," "Outline Proposal Sections," "Write Content," "Design Visuals," "Review & Edit." This step helps to bring order to the initial chaos, creating a higher-level structure that makes the project feel less overwhelming and more modular. It's like sorting a pile of laundry into darks, lights, and delicates before washing.

- **Break Each Phase into Smaller Sub-Tasks:** Now, take each major phase you've identified and break it down further into smaller, more manageable sub-tasks. The critical rule here is to make each sub-task small enough that it feels achievable in a single focused session, typically ranging from 30 to 90 minutes for an ADHD brain. If a sub-task still feels too large or abstract, break it down again. For "Book Flights," sub-tasks could be: "Research flight comparison sites," "Set budget for flights," "Check dates for best prices for specific routes," "Select airline based on criteria," "Input passenger information," "Complete payment." The psychological benefit of this step is immense: by creating these "bite-sized" chunks, you reduce the intimidation factor and create clear, approachable starting points that are less likely to trigger procrastination.

- **Define the "Next Action" (The Smallest Unit):** For every sub-task, identify the absolute smallest, most immediate *physical* action required to start it. This is your "next action." This step is paramount for task initiation, especially for the ADHD brain which can get stuck in "analysis paralysis." If you can't identify a physical action (something you can *do*), the task is still too big. It should be so simple that you can perform it almost without thinking, requiring minimal decision-making or mental energy to begin.
    - **Bad:** "Do taxes." (Too vague, overwhelming)
    - **Better:** "Gather tax documents." (Still a bit vague, what *exactly* do I do first?)
    - **Best:** "Find last year's tax return in filing cabinet." (Clear, specific, physical action) The "next action" is your clear starting pistol, removing the ambiguity that often traps the ADHD brain in a cycle of hesitation.
- **Estimate Time (and Add Your ADHD Buffer):** For each "next action" and small sub-task, estimate how long it will realistically take. Be generous with your estimates. As discussed in previous chapters, the ADHD brain often struggles with "time blindness"—underestimating how long tasks will take and how quickly time passes. To account for potential distractions, unexpected complications, or the need for a quick mental break, add a "buffer" of 25-50% extra time to your initial

estimate. If you think it will take 20 minutes, block out 30. If it's an hour, give yourself 90 minutes. This helps in realistic scheduling, reduces frustration when things take longer than expected, and builds a more accurate internal clock over time. Consistent overestimation is far less damaging than consistent underestimation.

- **Sequence Your Steps:** Once you have a detailed list of actionable steps and their estimated times, put them in a logical order. What absolutely needs to happen first? What steps are dependent on another step being completed? Use arrows, numbers, a simple outline format, or even drag-and-drop features in a digital tool to visualize the flow of the project. This creates a clear, sequential pathway from beginning to end, reducing ambiguity and showing you the logical progression. This structured view is incredibly supportive for the ADHD brain, providing a clear roadmap rather than a confusing tangle of possibilities.

Making It Actionable: Beyond the List

A beautifully broken-down list is useless if it just sits there, an elegant blueprint for inaction. The next critical phase is to ensure these steps lead directly to *action* and ultimately, accomplishment.

- **Use Visual Checklists:** Once broken down, transfer your actionable steps into a visual checklist. This could be a simple pen-and-paper list, a physical whiteboard, a digital task manager like Trello, Asana, Todoist, or a dedicated to-do app. The visual satisfaction of physically or digitally checking off small items provides valuable, immediate dopamine hits. These mini-rewards reinforce the positive behavior of task completion and build crucial momentum, which is particularly motivating for the ADHD brain. Seeing visible progress counteracts feelings of stagnation and overwhelm.
- **Schedule the "Next Action":** Don't just list the steps; integrate them into your calendar or daily plan. Block out specific time slots for those "next actions." This transforms an intention into a concrete commitment, creating external accountability and

reducing the cognitive load of deciding what to work on next. For example, instead of just "Research flight comparison sites," your schedule should read: "10:00 AM - 10:30 AM: Research flight comparison sites (Project Europe Trip)." This scheduled commitment provides a clear start time, minimizing procrastination.

- **Start with the Easiest or Most Appealing:** While logical sequencing is important, sometimes the best way to build initial momentum for the ADHD brain is to tackle the easiest, most appealing, or most novel "next action" first, even if it's not the absolute highest priority. This "easy win" provides an immediate burst of dopamine and a sense of accomplishment, propelling you forward into the more challenging tasks. It's a strategic form of "dopamine farming" that leverages your brain's natural tendencies to get started. Once you're in motion, staying in motion often becomes easier.

- **Focus on One Step at a Time:** Once you're working on a specific step, actively resist the urge to jump ahead, think about other parts of the project, or get distracted by unrelated tasks. Your current mission is *only* that one small, actionable step you've identified. Employ the single-tasking principles from Chapter 4. When your mind tries to wander to the next step or a different distraction, gently bring it back to the current, manageable action. When it's done, then (and only then) move to the next item on your sequenced list. This hyper-focus on the micro-task prevents the overwhelming feeling of the entire project from derailing your progress.

- **Acknowledge and Reward Progress:** Every time you complete a small step, take a moment to acknowledge it. Check it off with satisfaction. This small win provides a mini-burst of dopamine that reinforces the behavior and encourages you to keep going. Don't underestimate the power of these micro-rewards. They are the fuel for consistent motivation for the ADHD brain. This could be a mental high-five, a stretch break, a quick look out the window, or a small, pre-planned non-distracting reward. Over time, your brain will associate the feeling of completing a small step with positive reinforcement, making the entire process less of a struggle.

By consistently employing task breakdown, you transform overwhelming, nebulous projects into a series of manageable, psychologically less intimidating actions. You shift from being stuck at the base of a seemingly impossible mountain to confidently taking one well-defined step after another, seeing visible progress with each completed item. This clarity, systematic approach, and built-in reinforcement are fundamental to unleashing your productivity and consistently turning your ambitious intentions into concrete, satisfying accomplishments, paving the way for a more organized and effective way of working with your ADHD brain.

CHAPTER 3:

OVERCOMING PROCRASTINATION AND RESISTANCE

You've learned to break down tasks into actionable steps, a crucial strategy for managing the overwhelm that often paralyzes the ADHD brain. You've discovered how to transform intimidating "mountains" into manageable "hills," making projects less daunting and more approachable. Yet, even with a perfectly detailed plan, the invisible wall of procrastination and resistance can loom large, casting a long shadow over your intentions. This isn't a sign of laziness, a character flaw, or a deficiency in your work ethic; it's a common, often frustrating, symptom for men with ADHD, deeply rooted in how your brain processes motivation, reward, and the perceived difficulty or stimulation level of a task. It's a neurobiological hurdle, not a moral failing.

Procrastination, for the ADHD brain, often isn't about avoiding work altogether. Instead, it's a sophisticated, often unconscious, mechanism for avoiding the *discomfort* associated with initiating or engaging with a task. This discomfort can manifest in various ways, each signaling a specific challenge for your unique brain wiring:

- **Low Stimulation:** The task is perceived as boring, repetitive, abstract, or uninteresting, leading your dopamine-seeking brain to wander in search of more immediate novelty or engagement. The brain struggles to generate the necessary intrinsic motivation when the task itself doesn't provide enough external stimulation or an immediate reward.
- **Overwhelm:** Even a broken-down task can feel daunting if the sum of its parts still appears too large, too complex, or requires a sustained mental effort that feels beyond your current capacity. The sheer cognitive load of holding the task in mind, even in its smaller pieces, can trigger a shutdown response.
- **Fear of Failure/Perfectionism:** The desire to do something perfectly, coupled with an awareness of past struggles or perceived imperfections, can lead to paralysis. The perceived effort required to achieve an ideal outcome is too high, leading to an avoidance of starting altogether rather than risking imperfection. This is often an unconscious self-protection mechanism.
- **Difficulty with Future Self-Talk:** The "future you" seems capable of handling anything with ease, so the "present you" can comfortably defer the unpleasantness of the task. There's a disconnect where the consequences of inaction feel abstract and distant, making it easy to rationalize delay, believing that "future me" will have more energy, more time, or more motivation.

- **Time Blindness:** Without a strong, accurate internal sense of urgency, a deadline can feel distant and abstract until it's critically, overwhelmingly close. This makes it challenging to prioritize tasks based on their true time sensitivity, often leading to a reliance on last-minute adrenaline to kickstart action, a highly unsustainable and stressful approach.

Overcoming these internal barriers is fundamental to unleashing your productivity and transforming your intentions into consistent accomplishments. It requires a blend of psychological understanding, clever practical tricks, and consistent, compassionate practice that acknowledges and works *with* your ADHD brain, not against it.

Busting the Block:
Strategies for Overcoming Procrastination

The key to beating procrastination is to lower the activation energy required to start and to make the initial steps so small, so appealing, or so supported that your brain's resistance is minimized.

The "2-Minute Rule" (with an ADHD Lens):

This popular productivity guideline suggests that if a task takes less than two minutes to complete, you should do it immediately. For the ADHD brain, this can be a powerful starting strategy for low-friction tasks that don't trigger significant internal resistance. Quickly tackling tasks like replying to a quick email, putting away a single dish, or throwing out a piece of trash can indeed prevent a multitude of tiny tasks from building up into an overwhelming mental burden. The immediate completion provides a small, satisfying dopamine hit. **However**, it's crucial to acknowledge that even a two-minute task can feel insurmountable if it's boring, highly resistant, or lacks immediate novelty for your particular brain in that moment. If you find yourself consistently unable to apply this rule to certain "two-minute" tasks, don't view it as a personal failing or a sign you're "broken." Instead, it's a signal to apply deeper strategies: perhaps that specific two-minute task needs to be paired with something enjoyable, you need the presence of a body double, or it needs to be broken down even further into a *one-minute* or *30-second* step. The rule is a guideline, not a rigid law, and its effectiveness depends on the individual task and your current internal state.

The "Just Start" or "Tiny Task" Strategy:

Forget about finishing the whole project or even completing a large section. Just commit to starting the tiniest possible first step. "Open the document." "Read the first paragraph." "Type the title." "Write one sentence." "Send one email." "Put on my running shoes." This micro-commitment bypasses the brain's overwhelm response. The momentum generated by even this minuscule action is often enough to propel you forward, as the brain's reward system begins to engage with the act of doing. This strategy works because the "cost" of starting feels so low, it becomes easier to overcome the initial inertia.

Harness the Power of Urgency (Strategically):

Your ADHD brain often responds well to urgency, as the pressure can provide a much-needed dopamine boost. While relying solely on last-minute panic isn't sustainable or healthy, you can create artificial, controlled urgency to your advantage:

- **Set Micro-Deadlines:** For a sub-task or even a tiny action, give yourself aggressive, internal deadlines, even if the actual project deadline is far off. Use a timer (e.g., "I will complete this section in the next 30 minutes"). This creates a mini-pressure cooker that can help activate your focus and bypass procrastination.
- **Public Accountability:** Tell someone (a trusted friend, a colleague, a mentor, or an online support group) what specific task you plan to accomplish by a specific time. Knowing someone else is aware of your commitment can provide a powerful external motivator, leveraging social pressure to push through resistance. This can be as simple as a quick text: "I'm going to finish the first draft of that report by 3 PM."

"Pairing" or "Temptation Bundling":

Combine a dreaded or boring task with something you genuinely enjoy or find highly stimulating. This strategy leverages the ADHD brain's natural inclination towards novelty and reward.

- "I will only listen to my favorite podcast or a specific genre of music while I'm doing the laundry."
- "I will only eat this specific, slightly indulgent snack while I'm working on that tedious report."
- "I will only watch this new show while I'm on the treadmill." This associates a positive, immediate reward or enjoyable stimulus with the undesirable task, making the dreaded activity more palatable and easier to initiate. The brain learns to anticipate the reward, reducing the friction of starting the less appealing task.

Change Your Environment/Context:

If you're stuck in a procrastination loop, a simple change of scenery can be enough to break the mental block and signal to your brain that it's time for a fresh start. Move to a different room, go to a coffee shop, or even just shift your chair, stand up, or walk to a different part of your desk. This physical shift can create a mental reset, breaking the negative association with your current environment that might be contributing to the procrastination. It's a way to introduce novelty and signal a new beginning, which can be highly effective for the ADHD brain.

"Body Doubling":

Work alongside someone else, even if you're working on completely different things. Their mere presence, either in person or virtually, can provide a subtle sense of accountability, structure, and shared focus, making it easier to start and stay on task. The other person acts as an external executive function, providing a stable, non-judgmental anchor that helps to activate and sustain your own focus. Many online communities and apps offer virtual body doubling sessions, making this a highly accessible strategy. The knowledge that someone else is working nearby can significantly reduce the feeling of isolation and inertia.

Address the Underlying Discomfort:

When you find yourself procrastinating, take a moment to pause and honestly identify *why* you're resisting. Is the task genuinely boring? Does it feel overwhelmingly large? Are you afraid of making a mistake, or of the outcome? Are you feeling tired or overwhelmed? Acknowledging the specific discomfort allows you to apply a targeted strategy. For example, if it's overwhelming, break it down further. If it's boring, try temptation bundling or gamification. If it's fear of failure, remind yourself of "done is better than perfect." This metacognitive step empowers you to be a detective of your own procrastination, leading to more effective interventions.

Navigating Resistance: The Deeper Mental Blocks

Resistance goes beyond mere procrastination; it's a deeper, often subconscious, mental or emotional barrier that keeps you from engaging with important work, even when you logically know you should. It's the insidious internal voice that whispers, "You can't do this," "This isn't important enough," or "You'll fail anyway." These blocks often stem from past negative experiences, perfectionism, or internalized shame.

"Done is Better Than Perfect":

For men with ADHD who struggle with perfectionism, the pursuit of an ideal, flawless outcome can be incredibly paralyzing. The effort required to reach "perfect" feels insurmountable, leading to indefinite delay. Remind yourself constantly that a completed, even imperfect, task creates momentum, provides tangible progress, and allows for iteration and refinement later. Good enough, released, and in motion, is always better than perfect, perpetually stuck in your head or on your to-do list. This mantra combats the "all-or-nothing" thinking pattern that often traps the ADHD brain.

Externalize the Resistance:

Sometimes, just acknowledging and naming the resistance can lessen its power. When you feel that invisible wall, that deep reluctance, don't suppress it. Instead, externalize it: "Okay, I'm feeling a lot of resistance to starting this proposal right now. My brain is telling me it's too hard." Write it down. Speak it aloud to yourself. Acknowledging it without judgment helps you separate yourself from the feeling, allowing you to observe it rather than be consumed by it. This creates a small but significant cognitive distance, opening a space for choice.

The "Swiss Cheese" Method:

For tasks you truly dread or those that feel like an insurmountable block, don't try to tackle them head-on. Instead, "poke holes" in them. Spend just 10-15 minutes doing the easiest part, or a completely random small part, even if it's out of logical order. This breaks the intimidating solid block of the task, making it feel less formidable and more approachable. For a research paper, you might just find three sources. For a messy room, you might just clear one small surface. Each "hole" you poke reduces the perceived size and density of the "cheese," making the rest of it seem less daunting. This tactic capitalizes on your brain's need for small wins.

Embrace the "Messy Middle":

All projects, especially large ones, have a point where the initial excitement and novelty wear off, and the end isn't yet in sight. This "messy middle" is where many with ADHD abandon projects, as the dopamine hit from novelty fades. Recognize this phase as a normal, predictable part of the creative or productive process. Remind yourself that it's normal to feel less engaged, bored, or frustrated here. Instead of seeking a new, exciting project, double down on your tiny, actionable steps and leverage your accountability and reward systems to push through this phase. Knowing it's coming can help you prepare for it and not be derailed by it.

Self-Compassion and Reframing:

When you find yourself procrastinating or hitting a wall of resistance, avoid harsh self-criticism. Instead of thinking "I'm so lazy and undisciplined," try reframing it: "My brain is finding this task hard right now. What small step can I take to make it easier or more interesting?" Or "This resistance is a signal that I need a different strategy." Reframe procrastination and resistance as signals to adjust your approach or to apply a specific strategy, not as personal failings. Harsh self-criticism only triggers shame, anxiety, and a feeling of inadequacy, which further deplete the emotional resources needed for motivation and self-regulation. Cultivate an inner voice that is supportive, curious, and problem-solving, rather than judgmental.

Celebrate Small Wins:

The ADHD brain thrives on positive feedback and immediate reward. Don't wait until the entire project is finished to celebrate. Acknowledge and celebrate each small task completed, each tiny step taken, each moment of resistance overcome. This consistent, positive reinforcement provides crucial dopamine rewards that reinforce productive behavior and make future initiation and follow-through easier. Make it a deliberate practice: physically check off items, tell your accountability partner, or give yourself a pre-planned mini-reward. These small, frequent celebrations are the fuel that keeps your motivation tank from running empty during the long haul of productivity.

Overcoming procrastination and resistance is an ongoing battle, but one you can absolutely win by equipping yourself with these practical, neurobiologically informed strategies. By understanding *why* you procrastinate and by actively breaking down those barriers with targeted interventions, you'll unleash a powerful new level of consistent action, transforming your intentions into tangible accomplishments with greater ease, less internal struggle, and a profound sense of self-efficacy. This is about working smarter, not just harder, with your unique ADHD brain.

CHAPTER 4:

WORKFLOW OPTIMIZATION AND SYSTEM BUILDING

You've mastered breaking down tasks into manageable steps, a fundamental skill for bypassing the overwhelm that often paralyzes the ADHD brain. You've also confronted the insidious nature of procrastination and armed yourself with strategies to break through those invisible walls of resistance. Now, to truly unleash consistent, sustainable productivity, we need to move beyond individual tasks and focus on the bigger picture: workflow optimization and system building. This isn't just about doing more; it's about creating a streamlined, predictable path for your work, minimizing friction, and reducing the constant mental effort required to decide "what's next?" It's about creating an operating system for your life that supports your unique neurobiology, allowing your brilliant ideas and energy to flow effortlessly into concrete action.

For men with ADHD, a chaotic or unpredictable workflow is an enormous drain on executive function, almost like trying to run a race while constantly tripping over loose obstacles. Your brain thrives on novelty and excitement, but paradoxically, it also benefits immensely from underlying structure and predictability. Without clear, intuitive systems, every task becomes a fresh act of initiation, a new decision point, and an open invitation for distraction. This constant need to re-evaluate, re-prioritize, and re-locate information leads to:

- **Constant decision fatigue:** Spending valuable mental energy on *how* to do something, *where* to find information, or *what* to do next, rather than just doing the actual work. Each micro-decision drains your limited willpower and cognitive bandwidth, leading to exhaustion before you've even begun the core task.
- **Lost information:** Brilliant ideas, crucial notes, important documents, or pending tasks disappearing into the ether of a disorganized physical or digital system. This leads to wasted time searching, re-doing work, and the frustration of missed opportunities.
- **Inefficient transitions:** Wasting significant time and mental energy switching between different types of work, trying to locate necessary tools, or recalling where you left off on a project. Each transition becomes a potential derailment point for the ADHD brain.
- **A feeling of being overwhelmed by the sheer volume of "stuff":** Emails, physical documents, digital files, tasks, and fleeting ideas piling up without a clear home or a defined process for handling them. This creates a constant background hum of anxiety and the sensation of perpetually being behind, feeding the cycle of procrastination and avoidance.

Optimizing your workflow and building reliable systems isn't about becoming rigid or stifling your natural creativity; it's about creating freedom. It frees up your working memory by offloading information to trusted external systems, reduces the need for constant willpower by automating decisions, and provides a clear, well-worn path for your brilliant ideas and bursts of energy to flow into concrete action. It's about setting up the track so your ADHD brain can run on it with minimal friction, rather than constantly trying to build the track while simultaneously running the race. This intentional design empowers you to leverage your strengths, transforming potential chaos into structured efficiency.

Streamlining Your Flow: Optimizing Your Workflow

Workflow optimization focuses on the minute-to-minute, task-to-task movements of your work, actively reducing points of friction, eliminating unnecessary steps, and minimizing decision-making at every turn. It's about designing a smoother, more intuitive cognitive pathway for your daily tasks.

- **Define Your "Default State":** What happens when you finish a task? Without a conscious plan, the ADHD brain might default to checking email, scrolling social media, or getting a snack – activities that provide immediate dopamine hits but derail productivity. Instead, define a *productive* default for yourself: "When I finish task X, I will immediately check my 'Next Actions' list for task Y," or "I will review my schedule for the next pre-blocked task," or "I will do a 5-minute brain dump." This proactive definition reduces decision fatigue and creates a consistent, positive loop. By replacing a reactive default with a proactive one, you maintain momentum and direct your attention towards your true priorities.
- **Batch Similar Tasks:** Group similar activities together into dedicated time blocks. For example, process all emails at specific, pre-determined times (e.g., 9 AM, 1 PM, 4 PM) rather than reacting to each one as it arrives. Make all your phone calls in a dedicated block. Do all your "shallow work" (administrative tasks, quick replies, filing) at one time, and reserve your "deep work" (cognitively demanding tasks) for another, often earlier, block in your day. This strategy is incredibly powerful because it minimizes the mental "context switching" cost that is so draining for the ADHD brain. Each time you switch tasks, your brain has to reorient itself, load new information into working memory, and discard the old.

Batching reduces this overhead significantly, allowing you to build momentum within a single cognitive mode.

- **Create Checklists and Templates:** For repetitive tasks, recurring projects, or even complex one-off endeavors, create detailed checklists or templates. Whether it's for launching a new project, preparing for a weekly meeting, handling client onboarding, or even your morning routine, a checklist reduces the mental load of remembering every step and ensures consistency. Templates for emails, reports, or common documents prevent you from having to "start from scratch" each time. This is especially useful for preventing steps from being missed due to working memory challenges and provides external structure for reliable execution. Checklists effectively outsource the "remembering" function from your brain to a reliable system.

- **"One Touch" Rule for Information:** When you handle a piece of information (an email, a physical document, a note, a voicemail), try to process it, file it, or take an action on it immediately, rather than letting it sit and become "clutter." If it can't be dealt with in two minutes (as per the 2-minute rule), don't leave it in your immediate workspace. Instead, put it directly into your designated capture system (e.g., your inbox for later processing, a "to file" folder) to be reviewed and acted upon later. The goal is to minimize the number of times you touch or mentally process the same piece of information, reducing cognitive fatigue and preventing mental and physical clutter from accumulating.

- **Simplify Your Tools:** Resist the urge to use too many different apps, software, or analog systems. While the novelty of a new tool can be appealing for the ADHD brain, constantly switching between or managing multiple systems adds unnecessary complexity and cognitive load. Find one or two core tools for tasks, notes, and scheduling that you genuinely use consistently and that integrate well. The fewer systems you have to manage, the less mental energy is required to maintain them, ensuring reliability and reducing the chance of information falling through the cracks. Master your chosen tools rather than endlessly searching for the "perfect" one.

- **Review Your Workflow Regularly:** Your workflow isn't set in stone; it's a living system that needs periodic adjustment. At the end of each week (or even monthly), spend 15-20 minutes reviewing what worked well in your workflow, what caused bottlenecks or friction points, and what could be improved. Are there steps you can automate further? Can you eliminate unnecessary steps? Did you consistently follow your default states and batching strategies? This iterative process of review and adjustment is key to continuous improvement and ensuring your workflow remains optimized for your evolving needs and projects.

Building Your Foundation: Creating Reliable Systems

Systems are the underlying, often invisible, structures that support your optimized workflow. They reduce chaos, build predictability, and provide a trusted scaffolding for your executive functions. These are the habits and tools that prevent cognitive overload and ensure consistency, even on "off" days.

- **The Master Capture System:** You need one, and only one, reliable place to capture *all* your ideas, tasks, notes, commitments, and stray thoughts as they arise. This could be a single physical notebook that's always with you, a specific digital note-taking app (Evernote, Notion, Obsidian, Google Keep), or even a simple voice recorder. The key is that it's always available, easy to use, and you implicitly *trust* that anything captured there will be reviewed and processed later. This prevents valuable thoughts from being lost (which is a huge source of anxiety for ADHD) and immediately reduces mental clutter, freeing up your working memory. The capture system is the funnel for all incoming mental data.
- **A Consistent Review Schedule:** Having a capture system is useless without a rigorous, consistent review system. This is the crucial step where you process the captured information,

organize it, and integrate it into your actionable plans.

- **Daily Review:** At the start or end of each day, spend 10-15 minutes reviewing your capture system, processing new inputs, planning the next day's top 1-3 priorities ("Big Rocks"), and cleaning up any lingering tasks from the previous day. This ritual provides a clear start or end to your workday, helping with transitions and ensuring you wake up or go to bed with clarity.
- **Weekly Review:** This is perhaps the most important system for long-term productivity and stress reduction. Dedicate 30-60 minutes each week (e.g., Friday afternoon or Sunday evening) to conduct a comprehensive review of all your projects, commitments, and goals. Clear out old notes, process your email and physical inboxes, review your calendar, and plan the week ahead in detail. This holistic review is crucial for staying on top of everything, preventing overwhelm from accumulating, identifying potential bottlenecks, and ensuring your efforts are aligned with your overarching objectives. It's your personal strategic planning session.

* **Filing System (Digital & Physical):** A simple, intuitive, and *consistently used* filing system saves immense time, reduces stress, and prevents the feeling of being disorganized.
    - **Digital:** Implement a consistent, logical folder structure on your computer and cloud storage (e.g., by project, by year, by client). Crucially, favor search functions over overly complex, nested folder hierarchies. Learn to use the search bar effectively to find files quickly.
    - **Physical:** Implement a basic "Action" (for things needing immediate attention), "Archive" (for completed or reference items), and "Reference" (for frequently accessed information) system for physical papers. Don't let papers pile up on surfaces; process them into these categories immediately. Label clearly and consistently.
* **Scheduled Maintenance/Tidying:** ADHD brains often struggle

with ongoing, spontaneous organization. Instead of aiming for constant, unattainable tidiness, schedule dedicated "reset" times. This acknowledges that things will get messy and builds in time to address it. This could be 15 minutes at the end of each workday to clear your desk and digital desktop, 30 minutes every Friday to clear out email, or an hour on Saturday morning to reset your entire workspace and main living areas. By scheduling these resets, you prevent small messes from becoming overwhelming mountains, providing regular opportunities to refresh your environment.

- **Project-Specific Systems:** For larger, ongoing projects, create dedicated, centralized "homes" for all related information, notes, tasks, and communications. This could be a dedicated folder on your computer, a specific section or page in your note-taking app (like Notion or OneNote), or a simple physical binder. This prevents information from being scattered across multiple platforms and allows you to quickly dive into a project when needed, without wasting time searching for relevant materials or recalling context. All project-related items should live here.

- **Automate Wherever Possible:** Explore tools, apps, and software features that can automate repetitive tasks or reminders. This could include setting up email filters to sort messages, using scheduling tools for appointments, setting recurring reminders for bills or habits, or linking different apps with services like Zapier or IFTTT to create automatic workflows (e.g., a new email with a specific subject creates a task in your to-do list). Automation reduces the need for manual initiation and frees up valuable mental bandwidth, allowing your executive functions to focus on more complex, non-automatable tasks.

By investing time and effort in optimizing your workflow and building robust, reliable systems, you are essentially outsourcing decision-making and organization from your conscious mind to a trusted, external framework. This proactive approach significantly reduces the mental overhead associated with getting things done, allowing your focused attention and cultivated executive functions to be directed towards meaningful, high-impact work rather than fighting against inefficiency, disorganization, or constant cognitive friction.

This is how you create sustainable, powerful productivity for the ADHD brain, turning aspirations into consistent, tangible achievements.

CHAPTER 5:

REVIEW, ADAPT, AND ITERATE

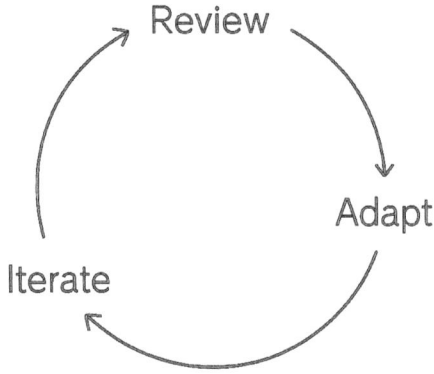

You've learned to break down daunting tasks into approachable steps, effectively dismantling the "impossible mountains" into navigable paths. You've also confronted the pervasive grip of procrastination and resistance, arming yourself with practical strategies to lower activation energy and initiate action. Furthermore, you've begun to build robust workflow optimizations and reliable systems, laying down the tracks for your productivity train to run smoothly. These are undeniably powerful steps toward unleashing your full productive potential. Yet, the journey to optimized productivity for the ADHD brain isn't a one-time setup, a static blueprint you follow indefinitely; it's a dynamic, continuous cycle of **review, adapt, and iterate**. Your brain isn't static, your life circumstances are constantly evolving, and neither should your productivity systems be.

For men with ADHD, rigid, inflexible systems often fail precisely because they don't account for the natural, often pronounced, fluctuations in energy, focus, interest, and the inherent novelty-seeking tendencies of your brain. What works perfectly one week – perhaps a specific time-blocking method or a particular environment – might feel impossible, boring, or utterly ineffective the very next. The novelty of a new system can wear off, the challenges of a new project might demand a different approach, or simply a shift in your internal rhythm can throw everything off balance. This is why a consistent, built-in practice of review, critical assessment, and strategic adaptation is not just helpful, but absolutely essential. Without this iterative loop, even the best-laid plans and most promising initial strategies can gather dust, lose their effectiveness, and the initial enthusiasm for new approaches can wane into familiar frustration and a return to old, less productive habits.

Think of it like a seasoned scientist in a lab, or an elite athlete training for a competition. They don't simply read a manual once and then execute blindly. They constantly experiment, observe the results of their efforts, collect data (whether informal or formal), tweak their methods based on what they learn, and try again with refined approaches. They learn as much, if not more, from what *doesn't* work as they do from what *does*. This iterative process of hypothesis, experiment, observation, and adjustment is how true mastery is achieved in any complex domain. For your productivity, it translates to:

- **Learning from experience:** Actively identifying what truly helps your unique ADHD brain thrive and what consistently creates friction, distraction, or overwhelm. It's about becoming an expert on *your own* operating system.
- **Catching issues early:** Preventing small problems – a forgotten task, a neglected inbox, a subtly draining habit – from snowballing into overwhelming chaos, missed deadlines, or a complete system collapse.
- **Refining your strategies:** Continuously making your systems more efficient, more intuitive, and more deeply personalized to your evolving needs, challenges, and strengths over time.
- **Building self-awareness:** Deepening your understanding of your own unique rhythms, triggers, energy cycles, and executive function fluctuations. This awareness is the foundation for genuine self-mastery.

This chapter will guide you through establishing a sustainable rhythm of self-reflection and proactive adjustment, ensuring your productivity strategies remain dynamic, effective, and perfectly tailored to your evolving needs, allowing you to consistently build on your progress.

The Power of Reflection: Why Review Matters

Regular, structured review periods are your brain's designated opportunity to pause, step back from the daily grind, assess what has happened, and recalibrate for what's next. They are the intentional moments that transform raw past experiences into invaluable future wisdom, providing the critical feedback loop that the ADHD brain often struggles to create organically.

- **The Daily Huddle (5-10 minutes):** This brief, powerful check-in can be done either at the very end of your workday (to close things out with clarity) or at the beginning of the next (to prime your focus). The key is consistency and brevity. During this time, take a few minutes to:
    - **Review yesterday:** What did you accomplish? Be specific. What did you *not* accomplish? Why? This is a moment for non-judgmental observation. Avoid self-criticism or dwelling on shortcomings. Simply notice the facts. Did a task take longer than expected? Was there a specific distraction?
    - **Identify wins:** Even small ones! What went well? Did you initiate a dreaded task? Did you stay focused for a solid 30 minutes? Did you remember to take your break? Acknowledging these micro-wins provides a vital dopamine hit, reinforcing positive behaviors and building self-efficacy.
    - **Note challenges:** Where did you get stuck? What was particularly distracting? Was a tool cumbersome? Was the task itself too vague? Pinpointing these moments helps you identify patterns for future adaptation.
    - **Plan your "Big Rocks" for tomorrow:** Based on your review, identify the 1-3 critical tasks that absolutely *must* get done tomorrow. This laser focus provides a clear

target for initiation and ensures you prioritize impact over mere activity.
  - **Clear your mental desktop:** Quickly process any lingering thoughts, unexpected tasks, or ideas into your master capture system. This prevents mental clutter from bleeding into your personal time or the next day, ensuring you start fresh.
- **The Weekly Recharge (30-60 minutes):** This is your strategic planning and clearing session, a non-negotiable appointment with yourself. Choose a consistent time that works best for you – perhaps Friday afternoon to close out the week, or Sunday evening to prepare for the next. This dedicated time is crucial for preventing overwhelm from accumulating and for aligning your actions with your larger goals.
  - **Clear the decks:** Process your email inbox to zero (or close to it), clear your physical desk, and tidy up your digital desktop (downloads folder, open tabs). This physical and digital decluttering clears the mental space for strategic thinking.
  - **Review all projects:** What's the current status of each project you're involved in? Are there any looming deadlines you overlooked? Are there dependencies you need to act on? This prevents "out of sight, out of mind" syndrome common with ADHD.
  - **Review your task management system:** Go through your master capture system, organize newly added tasks, delete irrelevant notes, update due dates, and add any new tasks that emerged from your project review. This ensures your trusted system is up-to-date and reliable.
  - **Assess the past week:** Beyond the daily huddle, take a broader look: What worked effectively this week in your productivity? What challenges did you consistently encounter? What strategies did you try, and what strategies fell flat? This is a deeper dive into patterns.

- **Plan the upcoming week:** Map out your "Big Rocks" and top priorities for the next 7 days. Schedule specific deep work blocks, allocate time for your "friction points," and deliberately plan for personal time, exercise, and rest to ensure balance.
- **Reflect on energy and mood:** How was your overall energy this week? Where did you feel most productive and engaged? Where did you feel drained, stressed, or prone to procrastination? This insight helps you refine your schedule to leverage your natural energy cycles.

- **The Quarterly Recalibration (1-2 hours):** Every three months, step back further for a broader, higher-level strategic look at your life and work. This prevents you from getting caught in the weeds and ensures your daily actions are still serving your long-term vision.
  - **Review your larger goals:** Are your annual goals, career aspirations, or personal development objectives still relevant? Are you making consistent progress toward them? Do they need adjustment based on new information or shifting priorities?
  - **Assess your systems:** Are your core tools (task manager, calendar, note-taking app, filing system) still serving you optimally? Do you need to try a new app, a different calendar view, or a fundamentally new approach to a recurring problem (e.g., managing specific types of distractions)? This is where you consider more significant changes.
  - **Identify recurring issues:** Are there patterns of procrastination, disorganization, or overwhelm that persist despite your daily and weekly efforts? What underlying causes can you identify and address at a systemic level? This might point to needing professional support or a more radical change in habit.
  - **Plan for the next quarter:** Set new, inspiring goals for the upcoming three months, refine existing ones, and consider new habits, strategies, or experiments you want

to implement to further optimize your productivity and well-being. This creates a fresh horizon to aim for.

Adapting and Iterating: Making Your Systems Agile

The purpose of these systematic review periods is not just reflection for its own sake, but purposeful, informed change. This is where you transform insights into action, making your productivity systems truly agile and responsive.

- **Embrace Experimentation:** Think of yourself as a kind of personal productivity scientist running micro-experiments. If a specific strategy isn't working for you (e.g., the Pomodoro Technique feels too rigid, or a particular app is too distracting), don't abandon the *idea* of systems altogether; adapt it. Try a different timer, a shorter or longer focus block, a different environment, or a new way of breaking down tasks. Frame it as: "This didn't work *for me* right now. What's one small thing I can change for next time to see if that helps?" This mindset removes the judgment and replaces it with curiosity and problem-solving, which is far more empowering for the ADHD brain.

- **Identify "Friction Points":** During your daily, weekly, and quarterly reviews, pay close attention to where you consistently get stuck, overwhelmed, distracted, or feel undue resistance. These are your "friction points" – the places where your intended workflow grinds to a halt. Examples include: constantly getting derailed by emails, struggling to start a particular type of task, or repeatedly losing track of certain documents. Once identified, brainstorm specific, targeted strategies to reduce that friction (e.g., if emails are a constant distraction, commit to closing the email client completely during deep work blocks, or uninstall it from your phone). The more precisely you can identify the friction, the more effectively you can address it.

- **"Just One Tweak" Mentality:** Resist the powerful ADHD tendency to try and overhaul your entire system at once when you identify a problem. Drastic overhauls are rarely sustainable and often lead to burnout and abandonment. Instead, identify just one or two small, actionable changes you can implement based on your review. Small, consistent improvements are far more sustainable and effective for the ADHD brain than large, disruptive revolutions. Think of it as chipping away at a statue: small, deliberate actions eventually reveal the masterpiece. A single new reminder, a minor change to your morning routine, or a different way to label a file can have a ripple effect.

- **Listen to Your Brain:** Your ADHD brain sends you constant signals – you just need to learn how to interpret them. If a task feels overwhelmingly boring, it might be too large and needs further breakdown, or you might need to pair it with a strong external reward or novel stimulus. If you're constantly forgetting appointments, you might need a more robust visual or auditory reminder system. If you're constantly losing focus, perhaps your environment needs more "noise" or less, or you need to experiment with different types of background sound. Pay attention to these signals of discomfort, frustration, or lack of engagement, and adapt your strategies accordingly. Your brain is trying to tell you what it needs to thrive.

- **Be Kind to Yourself:** This is arguably the most crucial element of the entire iterative process. There will be times when you fall off the wagon. Procrastination will reappear, systems will feel clunky, and you'll have "bad" productivity days or weeks. When this happens, avoid harsh self-criticism, shame, or guilt. These emotions are counterproductive; they deplete your mental resources and push you further into avoidance. Acknowledge what happened, observe it without judgment, learn from it, and gently guide yourself back to the process of reviewing and adapting. Remember that every successful man with ADHD has these moments. Self-compassion is not laziness; it is the essential fuel that keeps the iterative cycle going. It allows you to learn from mistakes without being crippled by them.

- **Celebrate Adaptation:** When you successfully identify a problem, brainstorm a solution, implement a tweak, and see it make a positive difference, take a moment to consciously acknowledge that win. This could be a mental high-five, a note in your journal, or sharing it with an accountability partner. This specific celebration reinforces your ability to learn, adjust, and solve problems, building profound confidence in your ongoing capacity for productivity. It provides the positive feedback loop that solidifies new habits and empowers you to continue the cycle.

By building in these consistent review, adaptation, and iteration practices, you transform your productivity journey from a rigid, potentially frustrating path into a dynamic, responsive, and deeply personalized process. You'll ensure your systems remain effective, perfectly tailored to your unique needs as a man with ADHD, and truly supportive of your overarching goals and aspirations. This continuous improvement is the ultimate key to unleashing consistent, powerful productivity, moving you from intention to accomplishment with increasing ease, effectiveness, and a profound sense of self-mastery.

CONCLUSION:
YOUR PRODUCTIVE POWER

You've journeyed through Book 3, "Unleashing Productivity: Turning Intentions into Accomplishments," and in doing so, you've gained a truly transformative understanding of how to harness your energy and focus to create tangible results. This book wasn't about conforming to generic productivity hacks, but about **redefining productivity for *your* ADHD brain**, building systems that genuinely support your unique way of working.

We've covered essential ground, from the foundational principles of:

- **Redefining productivity** to align with your strengths and natural rhythms, moving beyond conventional, often frustrating, metrics.
- Mastering **task breakdown** and identifying actionable steps, transforming daunting projects into manageable sequences that invite initiation.
- Developing powerful strategies to **overcome procrastination and resistance**, understanding the underlying mechanisms of these common ADHD challenges and providing practical solutions to break free.
- Implementing **workflow optimization and system building**, creating streamlined, predictable paths for your work that reduce mental effort and minimize friction.
- And finally, establishing a crucial cycle of **review, adapt, and iterate**, ensuring your productivity strategies remain dynamic, effective, and perfectly tuned to your evolving needs.

The true power of this book lies in its practical application. You now possess the knowledge and tools to consistently bridge the gap between your brilliant ideas and their real-world manifestation. You're learning to work *with* your ADHD, not against it, converting its unique aspects into an advantage. This isn't about becoming a robot; it's about reclaiming your agency, reducing overwhelm, and experiencing the profound satisfaction of consistent accomplishment.

Remember, productivity for the ADHD brain is a journey of continuous learning and refinement. Embrace the process of experimentation, celebrate every small win, and approach challenges with curiosity rather than criticism. Your ability to get things done, to move from intention to accomplishment, is no longer a roll of the dice; it's a skill you are actively honing, a powerful command you are exerting over your own productive potential.

As you continue forward, apply these strategies diligently. Watch how they transform your days, your projects, and your overall sense of self-efficacy. You now have the blueprint to unleash your authentic, productive power and consistently turn your aspirations into reality.

Let's pause for a moment and reflect on what you've just read. What resonates with you? What are the strategies you feel you can apply to work and life now versus those that seem more challenging or daunting?

BOOK FOUR:
MASTERING YOUR EMOTIONS WITH CBT TOOLS: NAVIGATING THE INNER LANDSCAPE

INTRODUCTION:
THE EMOTIONAL ROLLERCOASTER AND YOUR GUIDING HAND

You've worked diligently through strengthening your executive functions, sharpening your focus, and unleashing your productivity. These are critical external skills, but they often rest upon a foundational, yet frequently turbulent, internal landscape: your emotions. For many men with ADHD, emotional regulation can feel like an entirely separate and often more challenging frontier. While you might be able to plan a complex project, the sudden surge of frustration, the sting of rejection, or the overwhelming rush of excitement can derail your best intentions in moments.

Imagine your brain as a finely tuned sports car. Executive functions are the steering, brakes, and accelerator. But if the engine is running on highly volatile fuel, prone to sudden surges and stalls, even the most skilled driver will struggle to maintain control. For men with ADHD, that volatile fuel often comes in the form of intense, rapidly shifting, and sometimes dysregulated emotions.

This isn't a character flaw or a sign of weakness. Research consistently shows that **emotional dysregulation** is a core, often overlooked, aspect of ADHD. It manifests not just as difficulty managing "big" emotions like anger or sadness, but also as:

- **Emotional Intensity:** Feeling emotions more deeply and intensely than neurotypical peers.
- **Rapid Mood Shifts:** Moving quickly from one emotional state to another, often without a clear trigger.
- **Difficulty Soothing Yourself:** Struggling to calm down or recover from emotional upset.
- **Impaired Impulse Control Related to Emotions:** Reacting emotionally without a pause for thought, leading to regrettable words or actions.
- **Low Frustration Tolerance:** Giving up easily on tasks or goals when faced with even minor obstacles.

The impact of this emotional rollercoaster can be profound. It can strain relationships, undermine professional progress, lead to self-medication (e.g., overeating, excessive gaming), and erode self-esteem. You might find yourself saying or doing things you later regret, struggling with perceived criticism, or feeling overwhelmed by everyday stressors.

This book will provide you with a powerful guiding hand to navigate this inner landscape: **Cognitive Behavioral Therapy (CBT) tools**. CBT is a widely recognized and **extensively researched evidence-based**

therapeutic approach that has demonstrated significant effectiveness in helping individuals identify and change unhelpful thinking patterns and behaviors. While CBT is not a direct treatment for the core symptoms of ADHD, its components are highly effective for managing the emotional dysregulation, anxiety, depression, and stress that frequently co-occur with ADHD. It offers a structured way to develop skills for navigating emotional difficulties and building resilience.

It's not about suppressing your emotions or pretending they don't exist. Instead, it's about developing a keen awareness of your emotional triggers, understanding the connection between your thoughts, feelings, and actions, and building a robust toolkit to respond to emotions more effectively and constructively.

We'll start by exploring the specific emotional landscape of adult ADHD, then dive into practical CBT techniques for challenging distorted thoughts, implementing behavioral strategies for regulation, building emotional resilience, and fostering compassionate self-talk. This isn't a quick fix, but a journey towards greater emotional mastery, allowing you to move from reactivity to thoughtful response. Get ready to develop your guiding hand, transform your relationship with your emotions, and unlock a deeper sense of inner strength and peace.

CHAPTER 1:

THE EMOTIONAL LANDSCAPE OF ADULT ADHD

In the introduction, we touched upon the idea that emotions for men with ADHD can often feel like a dizzying, unpredictable rollercoaster, a turbulent ride through peaks of intense excitement and valleys of deep despair, often with sharp, sudden drops in between. Now, let's explore this "emotional landscape" in more detail, shining a light on the intricate ways your unique brain wiring processes and responds to the full spectrum of human feelings. Understanding how ADHD profoundly impacts your emotional experience is not about pathologizing your feelings or labeling them as "wrong"; rather, it's the first crucial step toward validating your lived experience, building self-compassion, and ultimately navigating your inner world more effectively and strategically. It's about recognizing the unique neurobiological underpinnings that shape your emotional life.

The traditional view of Attention-Deficit/Hyperactivity Disorder (ADHD) has historically focused predominantly on its "core" diagnostic symptoms: inattention (difficulty sustaining focus, being easily distracted), hyperactivity (fidgeting, restlessness, excessive talking), and impulsivity (acting without thinking, interrupting). While these are undeniably central to the diagnosis, a rapidly growing body of contemporary research, coupled with the consistent, often heart-wrenching, lived experience of countless men with ADHD, increasingly highlights that **emotional dysregulation** is a pervasive, profoundly impactful, and often debilitating aspect of adult ADHD. This means a significant difficulty in managing, modulating, and appropriately expressing emotions. It is so central to the daily struggles that many researchers and clinicians now argue it should be formally recognized as a core symptom of the disorder, or at least an intrinsic and highly significant feature. For many, it's the emotional turbulence, rather than the inattention, that causes the most significant distress and impairment in relationships, work, and overall well-being.

So, what does this nuanced and often challenging emotional landscape actually look like for men with ADHD? Let's unpack the key features:

- **Intense and Rapid Emotional Shifts:** Imagine your emotional thermostat is not just highly sensitive, but also lacks a robust internal "buffer" or dampening mechanism. While neurotypical individuals might experience a gradual build-up or fading of emotions, your emotional responses can flare up with startling speed and intensity. You might go from a state of calm to intensely frustrated or enraged by a minor inconvenience, then abruptly shift to profound boredom, followed by a surge of unbridled excitement, all within a remarkably short span of time – sometimes mere minutes. These dramatic and rapid shifts can be bewildering not only to you, leaving you feeling out of control of your own internal experience, but also to those around you who struggle to keep pace with your fluctuating moods. A small irritation, like a misplaced key or a delayed email response, can quickly escalate into disproportionate anger or a volcanic outburst. Similarly, a minor disappointment or perceived slight can trigger a deep, overwhelming wave of sadness or despair that feels all-consuming. This isn't simply about being "moody" or "overly emotional"; it's a genuine, neurobiologically-based difficulty in modulating the intensity, duration, and even the type of emotional response. The prefrontal cortex, often implicated in ADHD, plays a crucial role in emotional regulation, and its dysregulation can lead to a less filtered, more raw emotional experience.

- **Emotional Sensitivity to Rejection (often described as Rejection Sensitive Dysphoria - RSD):** This is a particularly painful, frequently misunderstood, and incredibly common characteristic experienced by a significant number of individuals with ADHD. You might find that even mild criticism, a perceived social snub, a hint of disapproval, or a sense of failure (even a minor one) can trigger an intense, disproportionate emotional storm within you. This isn't just feeling hurt; it's an immediate, overwhelming emotional pain that can feel physically agonizing, sometimes described as akin to being punched in the gut or stabbed in the heart. It's important to note that while Rejection Sensitive Dysphoria (RSD) is a widely recognized descriptive term and a profoundly impactful experience for many with ADHD, enabling them to articulate a previously nameless pain, it is not currently a formal, standalone diagnosis in official diagnostic manuals like the DSM-5. However, its profound impact on daily life is undeniable. RSD vividly describes the intense emotional pain and heightened sensitivity that stems from the *perception* (which is often more powerful than the reality) of being rejected, criticized, teased, or failing to meet expectations. This hypersensitivity can make navigating interpersonal relationships, professional feedback, and social interactions incredibly challenging, often driving compensatory behaviors such as intense people-pleasing, perfectionism (to avoid any perceived flaw), or social withdrawal and isolation (to avoid the potential for judgment or rejection altogether). The fear of this intense emotional pain can be paralyzing, leading to avoidance of situations that might trigger it, even if those situations are opportunities for growth or connection.

- **Difficulty with Impulse Control in Emotional Contexts:** Just as ADHD can manifest as impulsive actions (e.g., interrupting conversations, making spontaneous purchases, blurting out thoughts without filtering), it can also lead to impulsive emotional reactions. This means there's a shorter fuse between feeling a strong emotion and acting on it, with less time for the internal "stop and think" mechanism to engage. In the heat of an argument, you might blurt out hurtful words that you immediately regret. When frustrated, you might make rash decisions that have negative long-term consequences. When feeling overwhelmed or angry, you might lash out at loved ones or engage in behaviors that sabotage your own goals, simply because the emotional surge bypasses your internal brakes. The reduced inhibitory control associated with ADHD directly impacts your ability to pause, reflect, and choose a considered emotional response rather than a reactive one. This can lead to a frustrating cycle of impulsive emotional outbursts followed by profound regret and self-recrimination, further damaging self-esteem and relationships.
- **Chronic Feelings of Overwhelm:** The ADHD brain is often likened to a highly sensitive antenna, constantly bombarded by a multitude of internal thoughts and external sensory stimuli. This relentless input, coupled with inherent difficulties in executive functions such as prioritization, organization, working memory, and task management, can lead to a pervasive, enduring sense of being overwhelmed. This isn't just about having too much on your plate; it's a profound, emotional state where you feel flooded, mentally paralyzed, and genuinely unable to cope with the demands of daily life. Even minor stressors or seemingly simple tasks can trigger this feeling. When in this state, the brain often goes into a shutdown mode, leading to complete paralysis, avoidance of tasks, or emotional meltdowns when faced with situations that feel even slightly beyond your perceived capacity. This chronic overwhelm often contributes to procrastination, as the brain seeks to avoid the feeling of being flooded, even if it means delaying important responsibilities.

- **Struggles with Motivation and Emotional Energy:** While often discussed in terms of focus and task initiation, motivation has a profound emotional and neurochemical component, particularly for the ADHD brain. Your brain's dopamine reward system is crucial for motivation, and when tasks are perceived as boring, repetitive, abstract, or uninteresting, they struggle to generate sufficient dopamine for initiation or sustained engagement. This isn't laziness; it's a neurobiological reality. This can manifest as apathy, lethargy, a profound lack of emotional "oomph" for important but unstimulating activities (like paperwork, chores, or long-term planning), leading to chronic underachievement despite high intelligence and capability. Conversely, activities that are novel, highly stimulating, or intensely interesting can lead to "hyperfocus," an almost obsessive absorption. While hyperfocus can be incredibly productive, it often comes at the expense of other responsibilities, self-care, or other emotional needs, leading to an imbalance in emotional energy allocation. The inability to direct emotional energy efficiently where it's needed is a significant barrier.

- **Challenges with Self-Soothing and Emotional Regulation:** When intense emotions hit – whether it's anger, anxiety, sadness, or frustration – many neurotypical individuals have developed an unconscious repertoire of automatic coping mechanisms to calm themselves down, process the emotion, and return to a baseline state. For men with ADHD, these internal self-soothing skills can be underdeveloped, less effective, or simply not readily accessible in the heat of the moment. You might struggle to calm down after an argument, find yourself stuck in a prolonged loop of anxiety or resentment, or be unable to shift your emotional state even when you rationally know you should. This difficulty in internal regulation can lead to prolonged emotional distress, impacting sleep, relationships, and physical health. Without effective internal strategies, individuals may resort to less healthy external coping mechanisms such as excessive screen time, substance use, overeating, or other impulsive behaviors to temporarily escape or numb uncomfortable emotions.

Understanding these profound aspects of the emotional landscape isn't about making excuses for behavior, but rather about building a solid foundation for empathy, self-compassion, and most importantly, effective intervention. Recognizing that your intense emotional reactions, rapid shifts, or chronic overwhelm are often a direct result of neurobiological differences in your brain, rather than a personal failing, a character flaw, or a lack of willpower, can be incredibly liberating. It shifts the focus from "What's wrong with me? Why can't I just control my feelings like everyone else?" to a more empowering and actionable question: "How does my unique brain work, and what specific tools and strategies can I learn and consistently apply to manage it effectively?"

This crucial shift in perspective is the gateway to real change. In the following chapters, we will move from understanding to application, diving into specific Cognitive Behavioral Therapy (CBT) tools and techniques that directly address these emotional challenges. These tools will provide you with a structured, practical framework to observe your emotional patterns without judgment, challenge the unhelpful thought processes that often fuel emotional dysregulation, and develop tangible, actionable strategies to regulate your emotional responses. This will give you a guiding hand through your inner emotional landscape, transforming it from an unpredictable rollercoaster into a navigable terrain where you are increasingly in the driver's seat.

CHAPTER 2:

IDENTIFYING AND CHALLENGING DISTORTED THOUGHTS (CBT)

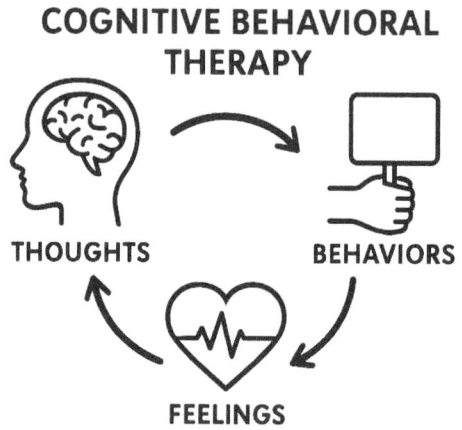

You've bravely begun to explore the unique and often intense emotional landscape of adult ADHD, understanding that feelings for men with ADHD can operate on a heightened, more rapid frequency. Now, we're going to dive into the first powerful set of tools from Cognitive Behavioral Therapy (CBT): understanding the profound, intricate connection between your thoughts, feelings, and behaviors, and learning to identify and challenge the distorted, unhelpful thoughts that often fuel emotional distress and dysregulation. This direct intervention on your internal monologue is a cornerstone of gaining greater control over your emotional responses.

The fundamental premise of Cognitive Behavioral Therapy (CBT), a well-established, extensively researched, and highly effective approach for addressing a wide range of emotional and behavioral challenges, is elegantly simple yet profoundly impactful: **your thoughts are not facts.** They are interpretations of reality, often automatic and unexamined, and these interpretations directly and powerfully influence how you feel and how you act. Decades of rigorous research have demonstrated CBT's efficacy in helping individuals learn to identify, evaluate, and ultimately change unhelpful thinking patterns, leading to significant and lasting improvements in mood, anxiety, stress levels, and overall well-being. The tools presented in this chapter are core components of CBT, widely used to build cognitive flexibility (the ability to consider multiple perspectives) and enhance emotional regulation by breaking the automatic link between a distorted thought and an intense emotional reaction.

For example, imagine a common scenario: you receive a critical email from your boss. The event itself is neutral; it's the *interpretation* of the event that dictates your subsequent emotional and behavioral response.

Scenario: Critical email from your boss.

Thought A (Distorted/Unhelpful): "I'm a complete failure. I can never do anything right. This proves I'm incompetent, and they're definitely going to fire me for this small mistake."

Feeling A: Intense shame, crippling anxiety, deep despair, a sense of hopelessness, perhaps even anger at yourself.

Behavior A: Procrastinate further on the task, avoid interacting with the boss, withdraw from colleagues, ruminate endlessly on the negative thought, leading to reduced productivity and increased stress.

Thought B (Balanced/Helpful): "Okay, this feedback is tough to hear. It points out an area where I can improve. What specifically can I learn from this? How can I implement this feedback and improve next time? Everyone makes mistakes."

Feeling B: Concern, determination, mild disappointment, a healthy sense of responsibility, but without the crushing weight of shame.

Behavior B: Review the email objectively, ask for clarification if needed, plan specific corrective actions, and perhaps schedule a follow-up conversation with the boss to discuss improvement.

The same external event (the critical email) can lead to vastly different emotional and behavioral outcomes based solely on your initial, often automatic, thought. For men with ADHD, who often experience rapid shifts in mood and intense emotional responses due to neurochemical differences (e.g., in dopamine regulation affecting motivation and emotional processing), these quick, often automatic, and unhelpful thought patterns are particularly impactful. Your brain's speed, its tendency to jump to conclusions, and its difficulty with emotional regulation can make you especially susceptible to these pervasive "thinking traps" or cognitive distortions, which then amplify your emotional rollercoaster.

Common Cognitive Distortions for Men with ADHD

Cognitive distortions are irrational or exaggerated thought patterns that reinforce negative thinking, undermine self-esteem, and exacerbate emotional distress. They are like mental shortcuts that, while sometimes quick, often lead you down a wrong path. Recognizing them is the first crucial step toward challenging them and reclaiming control over your emotional responses. Here are some common ones often experienced by men with ADHD, often amplified by the unique challenges of the condition:

- **All-or-Nothing Thinking (Black-and-White Thinking):** Seeing things in extremes, with no middle ground, no shades of gray. Everything is either perfect or a total disaster, a complete success or an utter failure.
    - **Example:** "I missed that deadline, so I'm a total failure and completely incompetent at my job." (Discounts all past successes and efforts). Or "If I can't do it perfectly, there's no point in starting it at all." (Feeds procrastination and perfectionism). This distortion often stems from the ADHD brain's tendency to struggle with nuance and moderation.
- **Catastrophizing:** Exaggerating the negative consequences of an event, jumping to the worst possible conclusion, even when it's highly unlikely.

- - **Example:** "If I forget to pay this bill today, my credit will be ruined, I'll go bankrupt, and I'll lose everything I own." (Turns a minor oversight into an apocalyptic scenario). Or "My partner looked annoyed when I spoke, so they must be furious with me, our relationship is irreparable, and they're on the verge of leaving me." (Often heavily linked to RSD, where perceived disapproval escalates to relationship termination). This is a common pattern when the ADHD brain's anxiety response is triggered, blowing a small issue out of proportion.
- **Mind Reading:** Assuming you know what others are thinking or feeling, usually negatively, without any actual evidence. This often involves inferring negative judgments about yourself.
  - **Example:** "My boss didn't say hello to me this morning and walked past without a smile, so he must think I'm doing a terrible job and is disappointed in my performance." (No evidence; boss might be distracted, stressed, or tired). This is extremely common and painful for individuals with RSD, as their sensitivity to perceived rejection makes them prone to jumping to negative conclusions about others' intentions and feelings towards them.
- **"Should" Statements:** Holding rigid, often unrealistic, expectations for yourself or others, often expressed with words like "should," "must," or "ought." When these expectations aren't met, it leads to intense guilt, shame, frustration, or resentment.
  - **Example:** "I *should* be able to focus for hours without any distractions, just like everyone else." (Ignores the neurobiological reality of ADHD). Or "I *shouldn't* feel so overwhelmed by simple household tasks; I'm a grown man." (Leads to self-criticism and invalidates your own experience). These "shoulds" are often internalized from societal expectations that don't account for neurodiversity.

- **Emotional Reasoning:** Believing something is true solely because you feel it strongly, treating your feelings as definitive evidence of reality.
    - **Example:** "I feel like a lazy, unproductive person today, so I must *be* inherently lazy and incapable." (Discounts effort and past accomplishments). Or "I feel incredibly anxious about this presentation, so it *must* be disastrous and I'm going to humiliate myself." (Ignores the possibility of performance anxiety and leads to avoidance). The intensity of ADHD emotions can make this distortion particularly compelling and difficult to challenge.
- **Overgeneralization:** Drawing a sweeping negative conclusion based on a single event or piece of evidence, assuming that if something happened once, it will always happen, or that it applies to all situations.
    - **Example:** "I messed up that presentation last week, so I'm terrible at public speaking and will never succeed in any leadership role." (One event defines entire capability). Or "My partner got frustrated with me for forgetting one thing, so I'm always going to disappoint everyone." (Exacerbates feelings of inadequacy).
- **Personalization:** Blaming yourself for external events or taking things personally that aren't actually your fault, or over-attributing events to your own actions.
    - **Example:** "Our team project failed because I didn't push hard enough on my part, even though multiple factors were involved." (Taking disproportionate responsibility). Or "My friend didn't invite me out last night; it must be because I'm boring." (Assumes personal blame without checking facts). This can tie into RSD, where any negative outcome is quickly internalized as a personal failing.
- **Disqualifying the Positive:** Ignoring, discounting, or dismissing positive experiences, compliments, or achievements, often by saying they "don't count" or were due to luck.

- **Example:** "I finished that tough project ahead of schedule, but anyone could have done it; it was just easy." (Minimizes your effort and skill). Or "My boss praised my work, but he was probably just trying to be nice." (Prevents genuine self-esteem from building). This distortion sabotages efforts to build self-worth and recognize progress, a key motivator for the ADHD brain.

How to Identify and Challenge Distorted Thoughts

The key to breaking free from the grip of distorted thoughts is to become a detective of your own mind. This is an active process of observation, questioning, and re-framing. When you notice a strong negative emotion, pause and investigate the thoughts that immediately preceded it.

1. **Catch the Thought (The "Pause and Observe"):**
    - When you feel a sudden surge of a strong negative emotion (anger, shame, intense anxiety, crushing frustration, deep sadness, acute self-criticism), use this emotion as a trigger. Ask yourself: "What thought just went through my mind right before I felt this way?" or "What am I telling myself right now about this situation or about myself?"
    - Write it down immediately, even if it feels silly or fragmented. The act of externalizing the thought (even briefly, on a sticky note or in a simple journal) helps you gain some crucial distance from it, allowing you to view it as an object of analysis rather than an undeniable truth. This is the first, most vital step in breaking the automatic emotional reaction.

2. **Question the Thought (The "Courtroom Test"):**
    - Once you've identified the thought, put it on trial. Imagine you are a neutral judge or a rigorous lawyer, meticulously examining the evidence for and against this thought. Ask yourself:

- "Is this thought 100% true? Is there *any* evidence to the contrary, no matter how small?"
- "What's the concrete evidence *for* this thought?" (Be specific and factual, not just general feelings or past assumptions).
- "What's the concrete evidence *against* this thought?" Are there other ways to interpret the situation? What might someone else, a neutral observer, see?
- "Am I falling into one of the thinking traps or cognitive distortions I just learned about?" (Refer back to the list above and identify the specific distortion: Is it all-or-nothing thinking? Catastrophizing? Mind reading?). Naming the distortion helps to depersonalize it.
- "What would I tell a friend in this exact situation if they came to me with this thought?" (We are often far kinder, more rational, and more compassionate to others than to ourselves).
- "Is this thought helpful? Does it move me towards my goals or away from them? Does it help me feel better or worse?" (A thought can be partially true but still unhelpful).
- "What's the absolute worst that could happen if this thought were true, and could I cope with it? What's the *most likely* outcome?" (Particularly for catastrophizing).

3. **Reframe and Replace (The "Constructive Alternative"):**
   - Based on your rigorous questioning, formulate a more balanced, realistic, and ultimately more helpful thought. This isn't about forced positive affirmations that feel untrue or saccharine; it's about finding a more accurate, nuanced, and empowering perspective that reflects reality more fully.

- **Original Distorted Thought (All-or-Nothing):** "I didn't finish everything on my to-do list today, so today was a complete waste and I'm a failure."
- **Challenging Questions:** "Is it 100% true it was a complete waste? What *did* I get done? Did I accomplish anything helpful at all? What would I tell a friend who felt this way?"
- **Reframed Thought:** "I didn't finish everything, but I did complete [X, Y, and Z important tasks], and that's solid progress. It wasn't perfect, but it wasn't a total waste. I'll re-prioritize for tomorrow and continue my momentum."
- **Original Distorted Thought (Catastrophizing/RSD):** "My partner looked annoyed when I brought up the chore list, they must be mad at me, and our relationship is in trouble; they'll probably leave me."
- **Challenging Questions:** "Did they *say* they were mad at *me*? Is there another reason they might look annoyed (tired, stressed from work, thinking about something else)? Have they been annoyed before and it resolved? Am I mind-reading? What's the evidence that our entire relationship is in trouble from this one moment?"
- **Reframed Thought:** "My partner looked annoyed. I'm going to take a breath and assume they might be tired or thinking about something else, or I can gently ask them later if everything is okay without immediately assuming it's about me or a catastrophe."

The practice of identifying and challenging distorted thoughts takes consistent, compassionate effort. These unhelpful patterns are often deeply ingrained, automatic shortcuts developed over a lifetime. But with persistent practice, you'll find yourself catching these thoughts earlier, questioning them more effectively, and ultimately choosing more balanced, realistic, and empowering interpretations of your experiences. This direct intervention on your thought patterns is a cornerstone of emotional regulation, giving you profound greater control over your inner landscape, transforming it from a turbulent, reactive space to one of greater clarity and intentional response.

CHAPTER 3:

BEHAVIORAL STRATEGIES FOR EMOTIONAL REGULATION (CBT)

You've learned to identify and challenge the distorted thoughts that often trigger and intensify emotional responses, equipping yourself with a powerful cognitive tool for emotional regulation. This internal dialogue intervention is crucial, but it's only half the equation. Now, we're shifting our focus to **behavioral strategies** – the practical, tangible actions you can take to directly influence your emotional state. While thoughts profoundly impact feelings, what you *do* in a given moment, how you move, or what you engage with, can also significantly alter how you feel, especially for the ADHD brain which often responds remarkably well to external action, physical change, and tangible shifts in its immediate environment or internal state.

For men with ADHD, emotional surges can be overwhelming, erupting rapidly and leading to impulsive actions, regrettable words, or prolonged periods of intense distress that feel impossible to escape. The brain's natural "stop and think" mechanism, which involves the inhibitory control of the prefrontal cortex, can be slower or less effective when emotions run high, leading to a shorter fuse and less time for considered responses. This is where behavioral strategies become your proactive toolkit, your first line of defense, and a powerful means of self-soothing. Instead of passively waiting for your thoughts to shift or for the overwhelming emotion to eventually pass, you actively engage in behaviors that can calm your nervous system, strategically change your focus, or provide a healthy, constructive outlet for intense feelings, preventing them from spiraling out of control.

Think of it like this: if your car's engine is overheating due to intense emotional build-up, challenging distorted thoughts is like checking the thermostat or diagnosing the problem with a diagnostic scan. It's essential for understanding the root cause. But behavioral strategies are like pulling over immediately, turning on the fan at full blast, adding coolant, or even temporarily shutting off the engine to prevent permanent damage. They are direct, actionable interventions designed to either reduce the immediate intensity of the emotion or shift your physiological and psychological state to a more regulated one. They give you concrete steps to take when your internal system is in overdrive.

Proactive Approaches: Building Your Emotional Toolkit

These strategies are most effective when practiced regularly and integrated into your daily routine. By proactively building these skills when you are calm, they become more readily available and effective when emotions become overwhelming. Think of this as preventative maintenance for your emotional well-being.

Mindful Movement:

We touched on this in Book 2 for sharpening focus, but it's equally, if not more, powerful for emotional regulation. Physical activity, even a brisk walk, stretching, a few minutes of jumping jacks, or dancing to a favorite song, can provide immediate relief from emotional intensity.

- **Discharge Energy:** Movement provides a healthy, physical outlet for releasing pent-up emotional energy, which is especially useful for managing anger, anxiety, restlessness, or frustration that often manifests physically in ADHD. It's a physiological "reset button."
- **Change Physiology:** Engaging in physical activity directly influences your body's state, shifting it from a "fight or flight" stress response to a more relaxed, parasympathetic state. It can reduce stress hormones like cortisol and increase feel-good neurotransmitters.
- **Shift Focus:** By concentrating on bodily sensations (your breathing, muscles, the feeling of your feet on the ground), movement redirects your attention away from obsessive or spiraling thoughts, grounding you in the present moment.
- **Action:** When you feel an emotion building, or you're stuck in rumination, take a quick, vigorous walk (even just around the block), do 20 push-ups, run up and down a flight of stairs a few times, or simply stand up and stretch powerfully. Don't overthink it; just move.

Scheduled Relaxation/Downtime:

For the ADHD brain, which is constantly processing stimuli and often running on high alert, the persistent internal activity can be profoundly exhausting, leading to emotional overload and burnout. Proactively scheduling genuine, restorative downtime is not a luxury; it's essential maintenance for your emotional well-being and a preventative measure against emotional dysregulation.

- **Action:** Block out specific, non-negotiable times in your day or week for activities that genuinely relax and recharge you. These are not "productive" tasks, but activities chosen purely for their restorative quality. This could be reading a physical book, listening to calming music, engaging in a non-demanding hobby (e.g., drawing, light gardening), spending time in nature, practicing a simple breathing exercise, or simply sitting quietly with a warm beverage. Treat this scheduled downtime with the same importance as a work meeting. This intentional emotional rest prevents your emotional "battery" from running completely flat, making you more resilient when stressors arise.

Sensory Grounding:

When emotions feel overwhelming, intense, or you feel disconnected and "in your head," engaging your senses can rapidly bring you back to the present moment, anchoring you to physical reality and interrupting the emotional spiral.

- **Action:** Use the **5-4-3-2-1 method** as a quick, portable reset: identify **5** things you can *see*, **4** things you can *feel* (e.g., your feet on the floor, the texture of your clothes), **3** things you can *hear*, **2** things you can *smell*, and **1** thing you can *taste*. This exercise forces your attention outwards. Alternatively, keep a "sensory kit" nearby: a stress ball for squeezing, a strong-smelling essential oil (e.g., peppermint, lavender) to inhale, a smooth stone or a textured fabric to touch, a piece of hard candy to taste. Engaging your senses provides immediate, tangible input that can override the intense internal emotional experience.

Structured Problem-Solving:

A pervasive sense of overwhelm often stems from feeling like problems are too big, too numerous, or too ill-defined to tackle. This can lead to emotional paralysis and increased anxiety. A structured approach to problem-solving can directly reduce emotional distress by providing clarity, a sense of control, and a pathway to action.

- **Action:** When a problem arises, instead of ruminating on it or allowing it to trigger a feeling of helplessness, take a few minutes to engage in structured problem-solving. Write down:
    1. **What is the specific problem?** (Define it clearly, concisely, and factually).
    2. **Brainstorm *all* possible solutions.** Don't judge them at this stage; just list everything that comes to mind, no matter how outlandish.

3. **Evaluate the pros and cons of each solution.** Consider feasibility, resources, and potential outcomes.
4. **Pick the best (or "good enough") solution.** Don't aim for perfect.
5. **Create a specific, actionable plan** for implementing that solution (breaking it down into tiny steps, as discussed in Book 3, Chapter 2).
6. **Set a specific time** to implement the action plan. This process shifts you from emotional reactivity and rumination to proactive, logical problem-solving, which is incredibly empowering and reduces the emotional burden.

In-the-Moment Interventions: When Emotions Run High

These strategies are for when you feel an emotional storm brewing, or you're already in the midst of one. They are designed for immediate, often rapid, application to de-escalate intensity and regain control.

The "STOP" Skill:

A powerful acronym from Dialectical Behavior Therapy (DBT), a close cousin of CBT, designed to create a vital pause between impulse and action, especially when emotions are overwhelming.

- **S - Stop:** Freeze immediately. Do not act on the impulse or say the first thing that comes to mind. Physically stop what you are doing.
- **T - Take a Step Back:** Mentally (and if possible, physically) detach from the immediate situation. Get some perspective. Take a deep breath.
- **O - Observe:** Notice what's happening internally (thoughts, feelings, bodily sensations like tension, racing heart) and externally (what are others doing, what are the facts of the situation). Be a curious observer, not a judge.

- **P - Proceed with Awareness:** After this pause, *choose* a deliberate action that aligns with your values or goals, rather than an impulsive, reactive one.
- **Action:** Practice using STOP whenever you feel a strong urge to react impulsively (e.g., interrupt, lash out, immediately buy something online) or when intense emotions unexpectedly flare up. The more you practice, the more automatic this pause becomes, giving your prefrontal cortex time to engage.

Distraction (Healthy Kind):

Sometimes, when emotions are too intense to process rationally or regulate directly, a temporary, healthy distraction can be incredibly helpful to prevent escalation and give your nervous system time to cool down. This is not avoidance in the long term, but a strategic, short-term pause to change your emotional trajectory.

- **Action:** Engage in a highly absorbing, short-term, and relatively neutral activity that pulls your attention away from the intense emotion: a quick, intense video game level, solving a simple puzzle, listening to a favorite upbeat song, watching a short, funny video clip, doing a quick, absorbing household chore (like washing dishes), or engaging in a brief, engaging conversation that is unrelated to the emotional trigger. The goal is to shift your brain's focus for 5-15 minutes until the emotional intensity drops to a manageable level, allowing you to then apply more direct problem-solving or emotional processing.

Radical Acceptance:

Some situations, and some intense emotions, simply *are*. Fighting reality or trying to force a different emotional response only increases suffering and perpetuates distress. Radical acceptance is acknowledging the reality of a situation or emotion without judgment, even if you don't like it or wish it were different. It's letting go of the struggle against what *is*.

- **Action:** When faced with an unchangeable situation (e.g., a past mistake, someone else's unchangeable behavior, an unavoidable outcome) or an intense, unwanted emotion, internally (or even aloud) say: "It is what it is," or "This is happening," or "I accept that I feel X emotion right now, even though I don't like it." This is not approval of the situation or emotion, but a release of the mental and emotional fight against reality, which paradoxically can significantly reduce distress and free up energy for more constructive actions.

Self-Soothing Through Senses:

Consciously and deliberately engage one or more of your senses in a comforting, calming, and pleasant way. This provides direct, physiological input to your nervous system, helping to de-escalate emotional arousal.

- **Action:**
    - **Sight:** Look at a comforting picture, watch something beautiful (a nature video, calming scenery).
    - **Sound:** Listen to calming music, nature sounds, or a soothing podcast.
    - **Smell:** Light a scented candle, use an essential oil diffuser, or simply smell a comforting scent (e.g., fresh laundry, coffee).
    - **Taste:** Drink a warm, soothing beverage (herbal tea, hot chocolate); eat a small piece of something comforting and savory; savor a piece of hard candy.
    - **Touch:** Take a hot shower or bath; wrap yourself in a soft blanket; pet an animal; put on comfortable clothing; hold a smooth stone. These are physical, tangible ways to calm your nervous system, directly impacting your emotional state.

Seek Support/Connect:

Don't isolate yourself when emotions are high or when you're struggling. Connecting with a trusted friend, family member, mentor, or therapist can provide perspective, comfort, validation, and a safe space to process intense emotions.

- **Action:** Reach out. A quick call, a text message, or even just being in the same room as a supportive person (without necessarily needing to talk about the problem) can help ground you, co-regulate your nervous system, and provide a sense of connection that reduces feelings of isolation and overwhelming emotion. Expressing your feelings to a non-judgmental listener can often help to diffuse their intensity and gain clarity.

By integrating these behavioral strategies into your daily life and having them ready for moments of emotional intensity, you build a powerful, proactive capacity for emotional regulation. This isn't about becoming emotionless or suppressing who you are, but about giving your guiding hand more control over your inner landscape, allowing you to respond to life's challenges with greater intention, resilience, and effectiveness. You are transforming your emotional rollercoaster into a vehicle you can confidently steer.

CHAPTER 4:

BUILDING EMOTIONAL RESILIENCE AND DISTRESS TOLERANCE (CBT)

You've learned to identify the thoughts that fuel your emotional responses and the immediate actions you can take to regulate intense feelings. Now, we're going to build on that foundation by focusing on **emotional resilience** and **distress tolerance**. These are crucial skills for men with ADHD, as the inherent challenges of ADHD—like managing daily tasks, social interactions, and professional demands—can often lead to chronic stress and emotional sensitivity.

Emotional resilience is your ability to bounce back from adversity, to adapt well in the face of stress, trauma, tragedy, threats, or significant sources of conflict. It's not about avoiding pain or never feeling negative emotions; it's about navigating them effectively and emerging stronger.

Distress tolerance is the capacity to endure and cope with uncomfortable or painful emotional states without resorting to impulsive, unhelpful, or destructive behaviors. For the ADHD brain, which often seeks immediate gratification or relief from discomfort, learning to "sit with" strong emotions is a powerful act of self-mastery. Instead of reacting to the intense urge to escape discomfort (e.g., procrastinating, self-medicating, lashing out), you develop the ability to ride out the emotional wave.

Think of it like building a mental and emotional immune system. You're not just treating the symptoms (intense emotions); you're strengthening your overall capacity to handle life's inevitable stressors and emotional challenges. This is particularly vital for managing the unique emotional landscape of ADHD, which can feel like living with an overactive internal alarm system.

Building Your Emotional "Immune System": Strategies for Resilience

Resilience is cultivated through consistent practice and a shift in perspective.

1. **Cultivate a Growth Mindset:** Instead of seeing setbacks or emotional struggles as proof of inadequacy, view them as opportunities for learning and growth. Understand that your brain can adapt and that challenges are a chance to strengthen your coping skills.
   - *Action:* After a difficult emotional experience, ask yourself: "What can I learn from this? What could I do differently next time? How did I handle this well, even if imperfectly?"
2. **Practice Self-Compassion:** For men with ADHD, harsh self-criticism often accompanies emotional distress. Self-compassion is treating yourself with the same kindness, understanding, and support you would offer a good friend in a similar situation. It's acknowledging your suffering and offering comfort, rather than judgment.

- *Action:* When you're struggling, place a hand over your heart and say to yourself (mentally or aloud): "This is a moment of suffering. Suffering is a part of life. May I be kind to myself in this moment."

3. **Build Your "Mastery" List:** Regularly engage in activities that give you a sense of accomplishment, competence, or pleasure, even small ones. This builds self-efficacy and a positive self-image, which are crucial for resilience.
   - *Action:* Make a list of enjoyable or mastery-building activities (e.g., solving a puzzle, learning a new skill, completing a household chore, exercising). Schedule time for these, especially when feeling down or stressed.

4. **Strengthen Your Support Network:** Isolation amplifies distress. Connecting with others provides perspective, empathy, and practical help.
   - *Action:* Nurture relationships with people who genuinely support you. Don't be afraid to reach out when you're struggling. Consider joining a support group or community focused on ADHD.

5. **Identify and Lean into Your Values:** When you act in alignment with your core values (e.g., honesty, creativity, connection, courage), you build a deeper sense of meaning and resilience, even when things are tough.
   - *Action:* Reflect on what truly matters to you. When faced with a difficult decision or emotional challenge, ask: "What would my values guide me to do here?"

Riding the Wave: Strategies for Distress Tolerance

These are "crisis survival" skills – techniques to get through acute, intense emotional moments without making things worse. They are about enduring, not necessarily solving the problem in that moment.

1. **Distract Wisely:** As mentioned in Chapter 3, healthy distraction can be a lifeline when emotions are overwhelming. It's about shifting your attention away from the distress until it subsides.

- Action: Engage in absorbing activities: solve a Sudoku, play a complex video game, watch a captivating movie, do intense physical exercise, or perform a quick, focused chore like cleaning.

2. **Self-Soothe with Senses (Revisited):** Consciously using your five senses to comfort yourself can calm an activated nervous system.
   - *Action:* Listen to calming music, take a hot bath, use an aromatherapy diffuser, savor a comforting food, wrap yourself in a soft blanket, or focus on a beautiful image.

3. **Improve the Moment:** Find ways to make the present moment more bearable, even if the underlying situation hasn't changed.
   - *Action:* Imagine a calming scene. Find meaning in the suffering (e.g., "This difficult experience is teaching me patience."). Focus on gratitude for something, however small. Take a few deep, slow breaths.

4. **Pros and Cons of Acting on Urges:** When you feel a strong urge to engage in an unhelpful behavior (e.g., yell, withdraw, impulsively spend), quickly list the short-term and long-term pros and cons of *acting* on the urge, and the pros and cons of *resisting* the urge.
   - *Action:* Write down a quick T-chart. Seeing the consequences laid out can often create the necessary pause for wiser choice.

5. **TIP Skills (for Intense Physical Arousal):** These are rapid physical interventions to quickly change your body's chemistry and calm intense emotions.
   - **T**emperature change: Splash cold water on your face, or hold an ice pack on your wrists/neck. This activates the dive reflex, slowing your heart rate.
   - **I**ntense Exercise: Engage in brief, intense physical activity (e.g., sprinting in place, jumping jacks, burpees) for 5-10 minutes to burn off excess energy.

- **P**aced Breathing: Slow your breathing. Inhale slowly for 4 counts, hold for 2, exhale slowly for 6 counts. This directly impacts your nervous system.
- **P**aired Muscle Relaxation: Tense a muscle group very tightly for 5-10 seconds, then completely relax it, noticing the difference. Work through different muscle groups.

Building emotional resilience and distress tolerance is a dynamic process. It's about learning to lean into discomfort with courage, knowing that you have a growing toolkit of strategies to navigate challenges without being swept away. By consistently applying these CBT-based tools, you are not just managing your ADHD; you are fundamentally transforming your relationship with your emotions, leading to greater stability, inner strength, and a profound sense of self-mastery.

CHAPTER 5:
COMPASSIONATE SELF-TALK AND INNER DIALOGUE

You've explored the emotional landscape of ADHD, learned to challenge distorted thoughts, and acquired powerful behavioral strategies for emotional regulation and distress tolerance. Now, we arrive at a critical, often underestimated, aspect of emotional mastery: **compassionate self-talk and your inner dialogue**. For many men with ADHD, the voice inside their head can be their harshest critic, amplifying anxieties, dismissing achievements, and reinforcing feelings of inadequacy. This internal monologue significantly shapes your emotional experience and your capacity for resilience.

Think of your inner dialogue as a constant conversation you're having with yourself. Is it a supportive coach, offering encouragement and guidance? Or is it a relentless drill sergeant, barking criticisms and fueling self-doubt? For men with ADHD, who often contend with a lifetime of perceived failures, missed deadlines, and impulsive mistakes, the inner critic can be particularly loud and punitive. This harsh self-talk is often a response to external criticism or internal frustration with ADHD symptoms, leading to:

- **Increased shame and guilt:** "I'm so stupid for forgetting that."
- **Reduced motivation:** "Why bother? I'll just mess it up anyway."
- **Heightened anxiety and depression:** Constantly reliving past mistakes or anticipating future failures.
- **Difficulty accepting compliments or successes:** "That was just luck."
- **Self-sabotage:** Unconsciously undermining efforts because of a belief that you don't deserve success.

The good news is that this inner voice is not fixed. Just as you can identify and challenge external negativity, you can learn to reframe your internal narrative, replacing harsh judgment with understanding and encouragement. Cultivating compassionate self-talk is not about being "soft" or ignoring your challenges; it's about building an inner ally who supports your growth, resilience, and emotional well-being.

Transforming Your Inner Critic into an Inner Ally

The goal is to shift from automatic self-criticism to conscious, supportive self-talk.

1. **Become Aware of Your Inner Critic's Voice:** The first step is simply noticing. When you feel a strong negative emotion or make a mistake, pause. What are you saying to yourself? What words, tones, or phrases does your inner critic use? Is it shaming? Demanding? Dismissive?
    - ○ *Action:* Keep a small notepad or use a voice memo to quickly jot down or record critical thoughts as they arise. This externalizes the voice and helps you observe it without judgment.

2. **Identify the Core Beliefs:** Often, repeated critical thoughts stem from deeper, underlying beliefs about yourself (e.g., "I'm not good enough," "I'm lazy," "I'll always fail"). Recognizing these core beliefs allows you to target them more directly.
   - *Action:* Ask yourself: "If this thought were true, what would it say about me as a person?" "What's the deepest fear or insecurity this thought touches upon?"

3. **Challenge the Inner Critic (Applying CBT from Chapter 2):** Use the same questioning techniques you learned for challenging distorted thoughts:
   - "Is this thought 100% true, or is my ADHD brain exaggerating?"
   - "What's the evidence *for* this thought? What's the evidence *against* it?"
   - "What would a compassionate friend say to me right now?"
   - "Is this thought helping me solve the problem or making me feel worse?"
   - *Action:* Write down the critical thought, then write down several compassionate, evidence-based counter-statements.

4. **Practice Self-Compassionate Rephrasing:** Once you've challenged a harsh thought, consciously rephrase it in a kinder, more understanding, and more helpful way.
   - *Original Harsh Thought:* "I can't believe I procrastinated again. I'm so lazy and useless."
   - *Compassionate Rephrasing:* "Okay, I procrastinated on this. That's a common ADHD struggle. What made this task particularly hard? What small step can I take now, or what strategy can I try next time?"
   - *Original Harsh Thought:* "I totally screwed up that presentation. Everyone thinks I'm incompetent."

- *Compassionate Rephrasing:* "That presentation was tough, and I felt like I struggled. It's okay to feel disappointed. What were my strengths in it? What's one thing I can learn for the next time?"

5. **Use Mindful Awareness to Create Space:** When the inner critic gets loud, practice mindfulness to observe the thoughts without getting entangled.
    - *Action:* Acknowledge the thought ("There's my inner critic again, saying I'm not good enough"). Imagine putting it on a leaf and letting it float down a stream, or observing it like a cloud passing by. This creates mental distance.

6. **Develop a Compassionate Inner Voice:** Actively cultivate a different voice.
    - **Use Positive Affirmations (that resonate):** Find short, truthful, and empowering phrases that counter your common critical thoughts. "I am capable of learning and growing." "My effort is enough." "I can handle this one step at a time."
    - **Imagine a Supportive Figure:** If it's hard to be kind to yourself, imagine what a wise mentor, a loving parent, or a supportive friend would say to you in that moment. Then, "speak" those words to yourself.
    - **Acknowledge Effort, Not Just Outcome:** Praise yourself for trying, for showing up, for taking action, even if the outcome isn't perfect. This is especially important for ADHD brains that can struggle with consistent output.

7. **Practice Gratitude for Your Brain:** Even with its challenges, your ADHD brain offers unique strengths: creativity, quick thinking, hyperfocus, resilience. Acknowledge these.
    - *Action:* Regularly remind yourself of the positive traits that come with your neurotype. This balances the narrative.

Cultivating compassionate self-talk is a continuous practice that slowly rewires your brain's default emotional responses. It builds a powerful internal resource for emotional resilience, allowing you to navigate the ups and downs of life with greater inner stability and self-acceptance. By transforming your inner dialogue, you transform your entire emotional landscape, becoming your own most reliable guiding hand.

CONCLUSION:
YOUR EMOTIONAL STRENGTH

You've now completed Book 4, "Mastering Your Emotions with CBT Tools: Navigating the Inner Landscape," and in doing so, you've equipped yourself with a profound understanding and powerful toolkit for managing the often intense emotional experiences that come with ADHD. This journey has not been about suppressing your feelings, but about developing a guiding hand to lead you through your inner world with greater awareness and control.

We've explored the unique **emotional landscape of adult ADHD**, recognizing that rapid mood shifts, low frustration tolerance (including Rejection Sensitive Dysphoria), and impulsive emotional reactions are neurological differences, not character flaws. This understanding is the bedrock of compassionate self-management.

You've then delved into the core CBT principles, learning to:

- **Identify and challenge distorted thoughts**, recognizing that your interpretations shape your reality and can be a source of significant emotional distress. You've gained the ability to question negative self-talk and reframe situations for a more balanced perspective.

- Implement powerful **behavioral strategies for emotional regulation**, from mindful movement and strategic relaxation to sensory grounding and the "STOP" skill, providing you with active ways to shift your emotional state in the moment.

- Build **emotional resilience and distress tolerance**, equipping you with the capacity to bounce back from adversity and to skillfully endure uncomfortable emotions without resorting to unhelpful behaviors.

- Cultivate **compassionate self-talk and a supportive inner dialogue**, transforming your harshest critic into a powerful inner ally who champions your growth and well-being.

The mastery of your emotions is not a destination, but a continuous practice. There will be days when the emotional rollercoaster feels more intense, and old thought patterns might resurface. This is normal. The true strength lies in your commitment to consistently apply these tools, to observe without judgment, and to choose a more intentional response.

You now have a clearer understanding of the interplay between your thoughts, feelings, and actions. You possess a robust set of CBT-based strategies to navigate intense emotions, build inner resilience, and foster a kinder, more supportive relationship with yourself. This emotional strength is a cornerstone of your overall well-being, enhancing your executive function, improving your focus, and profoundly impacting your ability to achieve sustained productivity and build meaningful relationships.

As you move forward, carry these insights and tools with you. Practice regularly. Celebrate your progress, however small. Your capacity for emotional mastery is growing, and with it, your ability to live a more balanced, fulfilling, and empowered life.

Let's pause for a moment and reflect on what you've just read. What resonates with you? What are the strategies you feel you can apply to work and life now versus those that seem more challenging or daunting?

BOOK FIVE:
ORGANIZATION, TIME MANAGEMENT, AND RELATIONSHIPS: CRAFTING A BALANCED LIFE

CHAPTER 1:

ORGANIZING YOUR PHYSICAL AND DIGITAL WORLD

You've put in significant work strengthening your executive functions, sharpening your focus, and developing emotional resilience. Now, it's time to integrate these hard-won skills into the practical realities of daily living: specifically, how you manage your surroundings, your time, and your connections with others. This final book, "Organization, Time Management, and Relationships," is about **crafting a balanced life** that genuinely works for the man with ADHD, moving beyond merely coping to truly thriving.

We start with **organization**. For many men with ADHD, the physical and digital world can feel like a constant battleground. Piles of papers, overflowing inboxes, scattered notes, and forgotten files are common culprits. This isn't a sign of laziness or a lack of care; it's a direct consequence of challenges with working memory, planning, and task initiation. Your brain's tendency to prioritize novelty over routine, and its difficulty with sustained focus on less stimulating tasks, can make maintaining order feel like pushing a boulder uphill.

The impact of disorganization extends far beyond aesthetics:

- **Lost time and increased frustration:** Constantly searching for misplaced items or information.
- **Missed opportunities and deadlines:** Important documents or emails getting buried.
- **Mental clutter and overwhelm:** A disorganized external environment often mirrors a disorganized internal one, adding to cognitive load.
- **Impact on relationships:** Frustration from partners or family members who struggle with the chaos.
- **Reduced productivity:** Inability to find what you need when you need it, leading to procrastination and delays.

The goal of this chapter is not to turn you into a minimalist guru overnight, but to help you establish **functional organizational systems** that reduce friction, support your executive functions, and free up valuable mental energy. It's about creating order that serves *your* brain, not a rigid system that you'll quickly abandon.

Taming the Physical Chaos: Strategies for Your Space

Your physical environment is a powerful cue. A cluttered space can signal "chaos" to your brain, while an organized one can prompt "clarity" and "focus."

1. **Start Small: The "Hot Spot" Method:** Don't try to organize your entire house at once. Pick one "hot spot" that causes you frequent frustration (e.g., your desk, the kitchen counter, the entryway table). Dedicate 15-30 minutes to *only* that area. This makes the task feel manageable and provides a quick win.
2. **The "One In, One Out" Rule:** For every new item you bring into your home (e.g., a new shirt, a new gadget), commit to removing

an old one. This prevents accumulation and forces conscious decision-making.

3. **Give Everything a Home:** Clutter often arises because items don't have a designated place. Assign a specific, logical "home" for every item you own. If it doesn't have a home, it's more likely to end up in a random pile.

4. **Containers and Labels:** Use clear containers, drawers, and baskets to group similar items. Label everything clearly. Labels reduce the mental effort of remembering where things belong and make it easier to put things away.

5. **Vertical Space is Your Friend:** Use shelves, wall organizers, and multi-tiered trays to maximize vertical space, especially on desks or counters. This clears horizontal surfaces, which tend to become dumping grounds.

6. **Regular "Reset" Sessions:** For the ADHD brain, consistent daily tidying can be tough. Instead, schedule short, regular "reset" sessions. This could be 15 minutes at the end of each workday to clear your desk, or 30 minutes on a Saturday morning to tidy common areas. This prevents small messes from becoming overwhelming.

7. **The "Landing Strip" Concept:** Create a designated "landing strip" near your entryway for essential items like keys, wallet, phone, and mail. This prevents frantic searches and ensures critical items are always in a predictable place.

Conquering the Digital Deluge: Strategies for Your Online World

Your digital life can be even more chaotic than your physical one, with endless files, emails, and notifications.

1. **Email Triage: The "4 D's" System:** Don't let your inbox become a to-do list or a storage unit. When you open an email, immediately decide:
    - **Delete:** If it's junk or irrelevant.
    - **Do:** If it takes less than 2 minutes to respond or action.
    - **Delegate:** If someone else needs to handle it.

- **Defer:** If it requires more time or attention, move it to a specific "To Do" folder or add it to your task manager.
- *Action:* Aim for Inbox Zero at least once a day, or at minimum, once a week.

2. **Strategic Folder Structure (Less is More):** Resist the urge to create endless nested folders. Keep your main folders broad (e.g., "Projects," "Clients," "Personal," "Archive"). Use a consistent naming convention. Rely on the search function for specific files; your brain is better at remembering keywords than specific folder paths.

3. **Cloud Storage for Accessibility:** Utilize cloud services (Google Drive, Dropbox, OneDrive) for important documents. This allows you to access files from anywhere and reduces the risk of losing them if a device fails.

4. **Desktop Declutter:** Your computer desktop should not be a holding pen for every downloaded file. Clear it regularly. Move temporary files to a "To Sort" folder, and permanent files into your organized folder structure. A clean desktop reduces visual noise and cognitive load.

5. **Digital Note-Taking and Capture:** Invest in one reliable digital note-taking system (e.g., Evernote, Notion, OneNote, Obsidian) to capture ideas, meeting notes, articles, and references. The key is to have *one* trusted place where you put everything, rather than scattering notes across different apps or physical scraps of paper.

6. **Regular Digital Backups:** Prevent the emotional distress of lost data by regularly backing up your important files. Use automated cloud backups or external hard drives.

7. **App Management and Notification Control:** Regularly review the apps on your phone and computer. Delete those you don't use. Turn off all non-essential notifications that constantly pull your attention.

By systematically applying these strategies to both your physical and digital worlds, you will create a more supportive and less distracting environment. This isn't just about tidiness; it's about reducing mental friction, making it easier to find what you need, and freeing up your precious executive function for more productive and fulfilling endeavors. An organized external world becomes a calm anchor for your often-busy internal world.

CHAPTER 2:

TIME MANAGEMENT STRATEGIES FOR THE ADHD BRAIN

You've begun to bring order to your physical and digital spaces, reducing external chaos. Now, we turn to an equally vital, and often more elusive, challenge for men with ADHD: **time management**. For many, time can feel like a slippery concept, an abstract idea that constantly eludes grasp. This isn't a failure of willpower; it's often a direct consequence of **time perception challenges (commonly referred to as 'time blindness')**. While 'time blindness' is a widely recognized descriptive term and a hallmark experience for many with ADHD, it's important to understand it's **not a formal diagnostic term**. Instead, it reflects a difficulty in accurately perceiving the passage of time, estimating how long tasks will take, or understanding the immediacy of future events. This neurocognitive difference makes traditional time management particularly challenging.

The impact of poor time management for men with ADHD is profound:

- **Chronic lateness:** Constantly rushing, missing appointments, or underestimating travel times.
- **Missed deadlines:** Leading to stress, poor performance reviews, and damaged reputation.
- **Procrastination loops:** "Plenty of time" quickly turns into "no time at all."
- **Over-scheduling:** Enthusiastically committing to too much, leading to overwhelm and failure to deliver.
- **Inability to prioritize effectively:** Everything feels equally urgent, creating a constant state of reactivity.
- **Increased anxiety and stress:** The perpetual feeling of being behind or out of control.

Effective time management for the ADHD brain isn't about rigid adherence to a minute-by-minute schedule. It's about developing strategies that make time more **tangible, predictable, and manageable** by leveraging your strengths and accommodating your challenges. It's about building awareness and creating external structures that compensate for internal time perception difficulties.

Making Time Tangible: Building Awareness and Estimation Skills

Your internal clock may be off, so let's rely on external cues and conscious practice.

1. **Use External Timers Liberally:** Don't rely on your internal sense of time. Use visual timers (like the Time Timer), phone alarms, or desktop timers for *everything*.
    - **Pomodoro Technique (Revisited):** As discussed in Book 2, using 25-minute focused work intervals followed by 5-minute breaks is an excellent way to structure time.

- **Time Blocking:** Dedicate specific blocks of time in your calendar for specific tasks or types of work. Treat these blocks as non-negotiable appointments with yourself.
- **Transition Timers:** Set a 5 or 10-minute alarm *before* you need to leave for an appointment or switch tasks. This provides a crucial buffer and reduces rushing.

2. **Practice "Time Travel" (Mental Rehearsal):** Before starting a task or leaving for an appointment, mentally walk through the steps involved and estimate how long each will take.
    - *Action:* For an appointment: "Okay, it's 10:00 AM. I need 5 minutes to grab my keys and jacket, 10 minutes to walk to the car, 20 minutes to drive, and 5 minutes to park and get inside. So, I need to leave by 9:20 AM." Compare this to your initial gut feeling.
3. **The "Actual Time vs. Estimated Time" Log:** For a week or two, keep a simple log. For every task, write down how long you *thought* it would take, and then how long it *actually* took. This builds crucial data about your personal time estimation errors and highlights patterns. You'll likely discover you consistently underestimate certain types of tasks.
4. **Visualize Time:** Use a large wall calendar or a visual planner where you can physically see your week or month laid out. Color-coding different types of activities (work, appointments, personal time) can further enhance this visual understanding of how your time is allocated.

Structuring Your Day: Optimizing Your Schedule

Once you have a better grasp on time, you can build a schedule that works for your unique brain.

1. **Identify Your Peak Productivity Times:** When are you naturally most alert, focused, and energetic? For many with ADHD, this is often in the morning, before stimulants wear off or before too many daily demands accumulate. Schedule your most challenging or important tasks during these "prime time" hours.

2. **Schedule Everything (Even Breaks and Transitions):** Don't just schedule meetings and work tasks. Block out time for breaks, exercise, lunch, deep work, shallow work (email, administrative tasks), and even travel. This creates a realistic view of your day and prevents over-scheduling.

3. **Build in Buffers (The ADHD Tax):** Always add extra time. If you think a meeting will be 30 minutes, block 45. If a task takes 1 hour, block 1.5 hours. This "ADHD tax" on time acknowledges your tendency to underestimate and provides crucial breathing room, reducing stress from constant rushing.

4. **The "Rule of 3":** At the start of each day, identify the top 3 most important tasks you *must* accomplish. Focus on these before anything else. This prevents getting bogged down in less important activities and ensures you move the needle on your priorities.

5. **Leverage External Accountability:** If you struggle to stick to a schedule, find ways to add external accountability. This could be a scheduled check-in with a colleague, a virtual body doubling session, or even just telling a friend your plan for the day.

6. **Review Your Schedule Daily:** Take 5-10 minutes each morning or evening to review your schedule for the next day. Adjust as needed, anticipate potential time conflicts, and mentally prepare for transitions.

Flexible Systems: Adapting to the ADHD Brain

Rigidity often leads to abandonment. Your systems need to be adaptable.

1. **Use Technology Wisely:** Utilize digital calendars (Google Calendar, Outlook Calendar) with alerts and reminders. Set multiple reminders for important appointments. Use task managers that integrate with your calendar.

2. **The "Park It" Place:** If you're in the middle of a task and a new idea or thought pops into your head, don't follow it. Immediately write it down in your designated "capture system" (from Book 3) and then return to your current task. This prevents derailment

while ensuring the idea isn't lost.

3. **Prioritize by Energy, Not Just Urgency:** Don't just tackle the most urgent tasks. Consider your current energy levels. If you're feeling low-energy, tackle a less demanding task that still moves you forward. Save your high-energy tasks for when you're at your best.

4. **Forgive Yourself and Adjust:** You will have "off" days. You will misestimate. You will get distracted. When this happens, don't beat yourself up. Acknowledge it, learn from it, and adjust your plan for the next hour or day. The goal is progress, not perfection.

By implementing these time management strategies, you're not just organizing your schedule; you're building a stronger, more reliable internal clock and a more realistic understanding of how you actually use your time. This mastery over time is a crucial component of reducing stress, increasing productivity, and ultimately, crafting a more balanced and fulfilling life.

CHAPTER 3:

NURTURING RELATIONSHIPS AND COMMUNICATION

You've made significant strides in organizing your environment and managing your time, two foundational elements for a more balanced life. Now, we turn to perhaps the most sensitive and profoundly impactful area: **nurturing relationships and communication**. For men with ADHD, the very traits that make you creative, spontaneous, and exciting can also present unique challenges in interpersonal dynamics.

The impact of ADHD on relationships is often underestimated, yet it can be a source of significant friction and misunderstanding. Common challenges include:

- **Difficulty with active listening:** Your mind might wander during conversations, leading to missed details or appearing disengaged.

- **Impulsive interruptions:** Blurt out thoughts or finish sentences, often without meaning to be rude.
- **Emotional intensity and reactivity (RSD):** Overreacting to perceived criticism or minor disagreements, leading to arguments.
- **Forgetfulness:** Missing appointments, forgetting important dates, or failing to follow through on promises.
- **Time blindness impacting others:** Chronic lateness or underestimating time for shared activities, causing frustration for partners or friends.
- **Task initiation in shared responsibilities:** Struggling to start or complete chores or shared projects, leading to resentment.
- **Hyperfocus on hobbies/interests:** Becoming so engrossed in your passions that you inadvertently neglect your partner or family.

These challenges aren't about a lack of caring; they're symptoms of a neurobiological difference. However, left unaddressed, they can lead to partners feeling unheard, unprioritized, or overwhelmed. The good news is that with awareness, specific strategies, and open communication, you can significantly strengthen your relationships and foster deeper connections.

Building Bridges: Strategies for Effective Communication

Communication is the bedrock of any healthy relationship. For ADHD, it's about being more intentional and strategic.

1. **Practice Active and Mindful Listening:** This is paramount. When someone is speaking to you, consciously turn off distractions (put down your phone, close your laptop). Make eye contact. Internally paraphrase what they are saying to ensure comprehension.
    - *Action:* Use the "Listen, Summarize, Clarify" technique: Listen carefully, then say, "So, if I'm hearing you right, you're saying [summary of what they said]. Is that correct?" This shows you're engaged and helps avoid misunderstandings.

- *Action:* If your mind wanders, gently bring it back to their words. It's a "rep" for your attention, as discussed in Book 2.

2. **Delay Your Response (The "Pause Button"):** Combat impulsive interruptions or emotional outbursts by creating a deliberate pause.
    - *Action:* When you feel an urge to interrupt or react, try taking a deep breath before speaking. You can even silently count to three. Or, if you absolutely have to say something, preface it with, "That sparks a thought, can I quickly mention it before I forget, then you can continue?" (Use sparingly).

3. **Use "I" Statements:** When discussing difficult topics or expressing emotions, focus on your feelings and experiences rather than blaming.
    - *Instead of:* "You never listen to me!"
    - *Try:* "I feel unheard when I'm speaking and you're looking at your phone."

4. **Schedule Important Conversations:** For sensitive or important topics, don't rely on spontaneous moments. ADHD brains can benefit from knowing when a difficult conversation is coming.
    - *Action:* Say, "I'd like to talk about [topic] tonight after dinner. Does that work for you?" This allows both parties to prepare emotionally and mentally.

5. **Externalize Your Thoughts (Respectfully):** Sometimes, your brain is just moving too fast. Learn to externalize without overwhelming your listener.
    - *Action:* "My thoughts are a bit scattered right now, but what I'm trying to say is…" or "I have several ideas popping up, let me try to walk through them one by one." This manages expectations.

Building Connection: Strategies for Relationship Nurturing

Beyond communication, specific actions strengthen the bonds in your relationships.

1. **"Time In" for Connection:** Schedule quality, distraction-free time with your partner, children, or close friends. This could be a regular "date night," a dedicated family activity, or just 15 minutes of uninterrupted conversation each day.
    - *Action:* Put these "connection times" into your calendar and treat them as non-negotiable appointments.

2. **Acknowledge and Validate Emotions (Especially for RSD):** When your partner or friend expresses an emotion, practice validating their feeling before offering solutions or explanations.
    - *Action:* "I can see why you'd feel frustrated about that," or "It sounds like you're really disappointed." This is crucial for navigating perceived criticism (RSD) from both sides – for you to validate their feelings, and for them to validate yours.

3. **Proactive Problem-Solving for Shared Responsibilities:** Don't wait for resentment to build over forgotten chores or shared tasks.
    - *Action:* Use visual aids for shared tasks (e.g., a whiteboard chore chart). Break down larger tasks into smaller, manageable steps. Schedule specific times for joint tasks, and use reminders. Communicate openly about what you can realistically commit to.

4. **The "5-Minute Burst of Appreciation":** Take brief moments throughout the day to show appreciation or affection. This could be a quick text, a genuine compliment, or a spontaneous hug. These small gestures add up.
    - *Action:* Make it a habit to verbally express gratitude or appreciation to your partner or family members at least once a day.

5. **Educate Your Loved Ones About ADHD (Gently):** Help your close relationships understand how ADHD impacts you, without making excuses.
    - *Action:* Share resources (like this book!). Explain *why* you might forget things or interrupt, and discuss strategies you're trying. This fosters empathy and can help them adapt their expectations or communication style.
6. **Manage Hyperfocus (Consciously):** If you're prone to hyperfocusing on hobbies or work, proactively communicate your boundaries or set timers.
    - *Action:* Tell your partner, "I'm going to work on this project for the next hour, and then I'll be done and focused on you." Use a timer to pull yourself out.

Nurturing relationships and improving communication for men with ADHD is an ongoing process of self-awareness, intentional action, and open dialogue. By applying these strategies, you'll not only reduce friction and misunderstanding but also build deeper, more resilient connections that enrich your life and provide invaluable support on your journey to a balanced existence.

CHAPTER 4:

SELF-CARE AND PREVENTING BURNOUT IN A DEMANDING WORLD

You've been diligently working on organizing your life, managing your time, and strengthening your relationships. This is significant progress! However, the very effort required to implement these strategies, coupled with the inherent demands of living with ADHD in a neurotypical world, can lead to a critical, often overlooked, challenge: **burnout**. For men with ADHD, the constant mental energy expended to focus, initiate, regulate emotions, and manage daily tasks makes you particularly susceptible to exhaustion, cynicism, and a reduced sense of accomplishment.

Burnout isn't just about feeling tired; it's a state of chronic physical, emotional, and mental exhaustion. It's often accompanied by:

- **Emotional depletion:** Feeling empty, numb, or overwhelmed.
- **Cynicism and detachment:** A growing sense of negativity towards your work, responsibilities, or even people.
- **Reduced efficacy:** Feeling less capable and productive, even if you're trying harder.
- **Increased irritability:** A shorter fuse and less patience with others.
- **Physical symptoms:** Headaches, fatigue, sleep disturbances, or increased susceptibility to illness.

For men with ADHD, these symptoms can sometimes be mistaken for worsening ADHD, leading to further frustration. The reality is that the constant effort to compensate for executive function challenges, navigate sensory sensitivities, and manage emotional dysregulation drains your internal resources at a faster rate. This is why **self-care** is not a luxury; it's a fundamental necessity for sustainable productivity and emotional well-being. It's the fuel that keeps your engine running.

This chapter will guide you through understanding the signs of burnout and implementing proactive self-care strategies that are specifically tailored to the needs of the ADHD brain, ensuring you can maintain your momentum and enjoy a truly balanced and fulfilling life.

Recognizing the Red Flags: Signs of Impending Burnout

Becoming attuned to your own unique burnout signals is the first step toward prevention.

1. **Increased Procrastination and Apathy:** You might find yourself avoiding tasks you once found manageable or even enjoyable. A general feeling of "I just don't care" sets in.
2. **Heightened Irritability or Emotional Blunting:** Small annoyances trigger disproportionate anger, or conversely, you feel a general numbness and difficulty experiencing joy or enthusiasm.

3. **Chronic Fatigue and Sleep Disturbances:** You're constantly tired, even after adequate sleep. Sleep patterns might become erratic, making it harder to fall asleep or stay asleep.

4. **Physical Manifestations:** Frequent headaches, muscle tension, digestive issues, or a weakened immune system (getting sick more often) can all be signs of chronic stress.

5. **Cynicism and Negative Self-Talk:** A pervasive sense of negativity about your work, colleagues, or even your own capabilities. The inner critic becomes louder and more relentless.

6. **Difficulty with Focus and Memory (Worsening ADHD Symptoms):** Your core ADHD symptoms might feel amplified – more distractibility, greater difficulty with task initiation, increased forgetfulness. This is your brain signalling it's overloaded.

7. **Increased Desire to Isolate:** Pulling away from social interactions or activities you typically enjoy.

If you recognize several of these signs, it's a clear signal that it's time to intentionally integrate more self-care into your routine.

Proactive Self-Care: Fueling Your ADHD Brain

Self-care isn't a one-size-fits-all solution; it's about finding what genuinely recharges *you*. For the ADHD brain, novelty and stimulation can be both a lure and a drain, so the right balance is crucial.

1. **Schedule True Downtime (The "Non-Negotiable Recharge"):** This is paramount. Just as you schedule work and appointments, schedule blocks of time for genuine rest and rejuvenation. This means *unplugging* from work, social media, and demanding tasks.

    - **Action:** Experiment with what truly recharges you: quiet reading, nature walks, playing with a pet, listening to music, engaging in a non-productive hobby (e.g., doodling, tinkering), or simply sitting quietly. Put these in your calendar.

2. **Prioritize Sleep Hygiene:** As discussed in Book 2, quality sleep is non-negotiable for ADHD brains. It directly impacts emotional regulation, focus, and energy.
   - **Action:** Establish a consistent bedtime and wake-up time (even on weekends). Create a relaxing pre-sleep routine (e.g., dim lights, warm bath, no screens 1 hour before bed). Optimize your sleep environment (dark, cool, quiet).
3. **Nourish Your Body and Brain:** Consistent energy levels are crucial for sustained effort.
   - **Action:** Focus on balanced meals with protein, healthy fats, and complex carbohydrates. Stay well-hydrated throughout the day. Be mindful of caffeine and sugar intake, as they can lead to energy crashes that exacerbate ADHD symptoms.
4. **Incorporate Movement Daily:** Physical activity is a powerful antidote to stress and mental fatigue. It helps regulate dopamine, reduces restlessness, and improves mood.
   - **Action:** Find an activity you enjoy and can stick with, even if it's just 20-30 minutes of brisk walking most days. Vary your activities to maintain interest.
5. **Set Realistic Boundaries:** The ADHD brain can struggle with saying "no" due to impulsivity or a desire to please. Overcommitment is a fast track to burnout.
   - **Action:** Learn to identify your capacity and politely decline requests that will overwhelm you. Protect your scheduled downtime and deep work blocks from intrusions.
6. **Delegate and Automate:** If possible, offload tasks that drain you or are highly repetitive.
   - **Action:** Delegate tasks at work or home where feasible. Explore automation tools for recurring digital tasks (e.g., bill payments, email filters). This frees up mental energy.

7. **Practice Mindful Breaks and Transitions:** Integrate short moments of mindfulness throughout your day to reset your nervous system.
   - **Action:** Use the "One-Minute Mindfulness Break" (from Book 2) between tasks. Before transitioning from work to home life, take 5 minutes to decompress – listen to a song, sit in silence, or do a quick stretch.
8. **Connect with Your Support System:** Social connection is a powerful buffer against stress and loneliness.
   - **Action:** Regularly connect with trusted friends, family, or a therapist who understands your experiences. Don't isolate yourself when feeling overwhelmed.
9. **Engage in "Flow State" Activities:** Activities that fully absorb you and provide a sense of timeless enjoyment are incredibly restorative.
   - **Action:** Identify hobbies or interests where you lose track of time (e.g., playing music, painting, gardening, specific video games, building models). Intentionally schedule time for these.

Preventing burnout is an ongoing, proactive commitment to yourself. It's about recognizing that your ADHD brain requires deliberate care and intelligent energy management. By consistently integrating these self-care strategies, you're not just avoiding exhaustion; you're building a foundation of sustainable well-being that will allow you to leverage your strengths, manage your challenges, and ultimately craft a truly balanced and fulfilling life.

CONCLUSION:
YOUR BALANCED LIFE, REDEFINED

You've now reached the conclusion of Book 5, "Organization, Time Management, and Relationships: Crafting a Balanced Life," and in doing so, you've integrated all the tools and insights from the previous books into a holistic framework for thriving with ADHD. This journey has been about much more than just managing symptoms; it's been about proactively designing a life that leverages your strengths, accommodates your challenges, and brings you a profound sense of equilibrium and fulfillment.

We started this book by addressing the practical, yet often overwhelming, aspects of daily living:

- **Organizing your physical and digital world:** You've learned to transform chaos into functional order, creating clear spaces that reduce mental clutter and support your focus.
- **Mastering time management:** By confronting "time blindness" and implementing tangible strategies, you've gained greater control over your schedule, reducing lateness and increasing predictability.
- **Nurturing relationships and communication:** You've acquired essential skills to listen actively, communicate effectively, and build stronger, more empathetic connections with your loved ones.
- And finally, in this last chapter, you've understood the critical importance of **self-care and preventing burnout**, recognizing that sustained well-being is the bedrock upon which all other successes are built.

The true essence of this book, and indeed this entire series, is the idea of **redefining success on your own terms**. For the man with ADHD, a "balanced life" isn't about achieving neurotypical perfection or adhering to rigid ideals. It's about:

- **Awareness:** Deeply understanding how your unique brain works and how it impacts your experiences.
- **Acceptance:** Embracing your neurodiversity, recognizing that your ADHD is a part of who you are, with both challenges and remarkable strengths.
- **Adaptation:** Continuously learning, experimenting, and refining strategies that genuinely support *your* specific needs and goals.
- **Action:** Translating insights into consistent, manageable steps that move you forward.
- **Compassion:** Treating yourself with kindness, understanding, and forgiveness throughout the journey.

You now have a comprehensive toolkit covering executive functions, focus, productivity, emotional regulation, organization, time management, relationships, and self-care. This is not a static manual but a dynamic guide. There will be days when strategies click, and days when you feel off-kilter. This is the human experience, amplified sometimes by ADHD. The power lies in your ability to **review, adapt, and iterate**, as you learned in Book 3.

As you step forward, carry the confidence that comes from knowledge and practical application. You are not just managing ADHD; you are actively *crafting* a life that allows you to flourish. Your unique blend of creativity, spontaneity, and energy, when supported by these learned skills, becomes a powerful force for innovation and connection.

Embrace the ongoing journey. Celebrate your resilience. Trust in your growing capacity for self-mastery. Your balanced life, redefined and purposefully built, awaits.

Let's pause for a moment and reflect on what you've just read. What resonates with you? What are the strategies you feel you can apply to work and life now versus those that seem more challenging or daunting?

OVERALL CONCLUSION:
THE EMPOWERED MAN WITH ADHD

You've journeyed through this comprehensive five-book series, dedicating yourself to understanding, adapting, and ultimately thriving with ADHD. This isn't just a collection of strategies; it's a profound transformation of how you relate to your own neurobiology and engage with the world around you.

From the foundational executive functions, through the intricacies of focus and productivity, navigating your emotional landscape, and finally, crafting a balanced life — you've actively built a robust framework for success on your own terms. You've come to understand that **ADHD isn't a deficit to be cured, but a unique operating system to be mastered.**

This series has armed you with:

- **Self-Awareness:** A deep understanding of how your brain works, its strengths, its challenges, and its unique rhythms. This insight is the foundation of all effective self-management.
- **Actionable Strategies:** Concrete, practical tools across all vital areas of life, designed to work *with* your ADHD brain, not against it.
- **Emotional Resilience:** The capacity to navigate intense feelings, challenge distorted thoughts, and cultivate an inner dialogue that supports, rather than sabotages, your well-being.
- **System Building:** The ability to create external structures that compensate for internal challenges, reducing friction and freeing up mental energy for what truly matters.
- **Self-Compassion:** The crucial understanding that progress, not perfection, is the goal, and that kindness toward yourself is the most powerful catalyst for sustainable change.

You are no longer merely coping with ADHD; you are actively **crafting a life that is aligned with your unique strengths and values.** You are becoming the architect of your own experience, making intentional choices rather than being swept away by distraction, procrastination, or emotional turbulence.

The journey continues, of course. Life is dynamic, and so are the demands placed upon you. There will be new challenges, moments of overwhelm, and times when you may temporarily fall back on old habits. This is normal. The true power lies in your newfound ability to:

- **Recognize** when you're struggling.
- **Refer** back to your toolkit.
- **Re-engage** with the strategies that work for you.
- **Review, Adapt, and Iterate** your approach, always learning and evolving.

You are now an **Empowered Man with ADHD.** You possess the knowledge, the skills, and the mindset to navigate your world with greater clarity, purpose, and peace. Embrace your neurodiversity, celebrate your unique gifts, and continue to build the extraordinary life you are capable of living.

- *An additional note: Although this book is titled as being geared towards the needs of men with ADHD, it can be used by women too.*

www.ingramcontent.com/pod-product-compliance
Lightning Source LLC
Chambersburg PA
CBHW070327010526
44107CB00004B/444